C-872 CAREER EXAMINATION SERIES

This is your PASSBOOK for...

Warehouse and Toolroom Worker

Test Preparation Study Guide
Questions & Answers

NLC®

NATIONAL LEARNING CORPORATION®

COPYRIGHT NOTICE

National Learning Corporation

212 Michael Drive, Syosset, NY 11791
(516) 921-8888 • www.passbooks.com
E-mail: info@passbooks.com

PASSBOOK® SERIES

THE *PASSBOOK® SERIES* has been created to prepare applicants and candidates for the ultimate academic battlefield – the examination room.

At some time in our lives, each and every one of us may be required to take an examination – for validation, matriculation, admission, qualification, registration, certification, or licensure.

Based on the assumption that every applicant or candidate has met the basic formal educational standards, has taken the required number of courses, and read the necessary texts, the *PASSBOOK® SERIES* furnishes the one special preparation which may assure passing with confidence, instead of failing with insecurity. Examination questions – together with answers – are furnished as the basic vehicle for study so that the mysteries of the examination and its compounding difficulties may be eliminated or diminished by a sure method.

This book is meant to help you pass your examination provided that you qualify and are serious in your objective.

The entire field is reviewed through the huge store of content information which is succinctly presented through a provocative and challenging approach – the question-and-answer method.

A climate of success is established by furnishing the correct answers at the end of each test.

You soon learn to recognize types of questions, forms of questions, and patterns of questioning. You may even begin to anticipate expected outcomes.

You perceive that many questions are repeated or adapted so that you can gain acute insights, which may enable you to score many sure points.

You learn how to confront new questions, or types of questions, and to attack them confidently and work out the correct answers.

You note objectives and emphases, and recognize pitfalls and dangers, so that you may make positive educational adjustments.

Moreover, you are kept fully informed in relation to new concepts, methods, practices, and directions in the field.

You discover that you are actually taking the examination all the time: you are preparing for the examination by "taking" an examination, not by reading extraneous and/or supererogatory textbooks.

In short, this PASSBOOK®, used directedly, should be an important factor in helping you to pass your test.

WAREHOUSE AND TOOLROOM WORKER

DUTIES:

A Warehouse and Toolroom Worker performs manual and clerical work in ordering, receiving, storing, issuing, and accounting for materials, supplies, automotive parts, tools, and equipment; may be required to lift boxes, load, and unload trucks, package materials and make supply deliveries; may operate motor-driven and various material handling and lifting equipment, including forklifts, jacks, and hoists. May perform minor repair, maintenance, and assembly on tools, equipment and materials; and does related work.

SCOPE OF THE EXAMINATION:

The examination will consist entirely of a multiple-choice test. In the multiple-choice test, the following competencies may be evaluated: reading comprehension; mathematics; safety focus including safety procedures and guidelines specific to driving and traffic safety hand signals; handling, moving and storing of hazardous substances; reviewing safety data sheets; and use of personal protective equipment; customer service; teamwork; and job knowledge including knowledge of: proper packing procedures sufficient to efficiently box, pack, store, and/or prepare supplies; standard abbreviations for liquid measurements and units of issue and order sufficient to designate weights and measures, verify deliveries, check stock, and provide materials to field personnel in the requested amount; common clerical practices such as filing in alphabetical, chronological and numerical order sufficient to organize and maintain hard copy files in a clear and understandable manner; various types of manual and power tools, equipment, and materials commonly found in warehouses, toolrooms, or supply rooms; rigging procedures and various types of tools, and equipment used to move materials of differing sizes, shapes, and types; and other necessary skills, knowledge, and abilities.

HOW TO TAKE A TEST

I. YOU MUST PASS AN EXAMINATION

A. WHAT EVERY CANDIDATE SHOULD KNOW

Examination applicants often ask us for help in preparing for the written test. What can I study in advance? What kinds of questions will be asked? How will the test be given? How will the papers be graded?

As an applicant for a civil service examination, you may be wondering about some of these things. Our purpose here is to suggest effective methods of advance study and to describe civil service examinations.

Your chances for success on this examination can be increased if you know how to prepare. Those "pre-examination jitters" can be reduced if you know what to expect. You can even experience an adventure in good citizenship if you know why civil service exams are given.

B. WHY ARE CIVIL SERVICE EXAMINATIONS GIVEN?

Civil service examinations are important to you in two ways. As a citizen, you want public jobs filled by employees who know how to do their work. As a job seeker, you want a fair chance to compete for that job on an equal footing with other candidates. The best-known means of accomplishing this two-fold goal is the competitive examination.

Exams are widely publicized throughout the nation. They may be administered for jobs in federal, state, city, municipal, town or village governments or agencies.

Any citizen may apply, with some limitations, such as the age or residence of applicants. Your experience and education may be reviewed to see whether you meet the requirements for the particular examination. When these requirements exist, they are reasonable and applied consistently to all applicants. Thus, a competitive examination may cause you some uneasiness now, but it is your privilege and safeguard.

C. HOW ARE CIVIL SERVICE EXAMS DEVELOPED?

Examinations are carefully written by trained technicians who are specialists in the field known as "psychological measurement," in consultation with recognized authorities in the field of work that the test will cover. These experts recommend the subject matter areas or skills to be tested; only those knowledges or skills important to your success on the job are included. The most reliable books and source materials available are used as references. Together, the experts and technicians judge the difficulty level of the questions.

Test technicians know how to phrase questions so that the problem is clearly stated. Their ethics do not permit "trick" or "catch" questions. Questions may have been tried out on sample groups, or subjected to statistical analysis, to determine their usefulness.

Written tests are often used in combination with performance tests, ratings of training and experience, and oral interviews. All of these measures combine to form the best-known means of finding the right person for the right job.

II. HOW TO PASS THE WRITTEN TEST

A. NATURE OF THE EXAMINATION

To prepare intelligently for civil service examinations, you should know how they differ from school examinations you have taken. In school you were assigned certain definite pages to read or subjects to cover. The examination questions were quite detailed and usually emphasized memory. Civil service exams, on the other hand, try to discover your present ability to perform the duties of a position, plus your potentiality to learn these duties. In other words, a civil service exam attempts to predict how successful you will be. Questions cover such a broad area that they cannot be as minute and detailed as school exam questions.

In the public service similar kinds of work, or positions, are grouped together in one "class." This process is known as *position-classification.* All the positions in a class are paid according to the salary range for that class. One class title covers all of these positions, and they are all tested by the same examination.

B. FOUR BASIC STEPS

1) Study the announcement

How, then, can you know what subjects to study? Our best answer is: "Learn as much as possible about the class of positions for which you've applied." The exam will test the knowledge, skills and abilities needed to do the work.

Your most valuable source of information about the position you want is the official exam announcement. This announcement lists the training and experience qualifications. Check these standards and apply only if you come reasonably close to meeting them.

The brief description of the position in the examination announcement offers some clues to the subjects which will be tested. Think about the job itself. Review the duties in your mind. Can you perform them, or are there some in which you are rusty? Fill in the blank spots in your preparation.

Many jurisdictions preview the written test in the exam announcement by including a section called "Knowledge and Abilities Required," "Scope of the Examination," or some similar heading. Here you will find out specifically what fields will be tested.

2) Review your own background

Once you learn in general what the position is all about, and what you need to know to do the work, ask yourself which subjects you already know fairly well and which need improvement. You may wonder whether to concentrate on improving your strong areas or on building some background in your fields of weakness. When the announcement has specified "some knowledge" or "considerable knowledge," or has used adjectives like "beginning principles of..." or "advanced ... methods," you can get a clue as to the number and difficulty of questions to be asked in any given field. More questions, and hence broader coverage, would be included for those subjects which are more important in the work. Now weigh your strengths and weaknesses against the job requirements and prepare accordingly.

3) Determine the level of the position

Another way to tell how intensively you should prepare is to understand the level of the job for which you are applying. Is it the entering level? In other words, is this the position in which beginners in a field of work are hired? Or is it an intermediate or advanced level? Sometimes this is indicated by such words as "Junior" or "Senior" in the class title. Other jurisdictions use Roman numerals to designate the level – Clerk I, Clerk II, for example. The word "Supervisor" sometimes appears in the title. If the level is not indicated by the title, check the description of duties. Will you be working under very close supervision, or will you have responsibility for independent decisions in this work?

4) Choose appropriate study materials

Now that you know the subjects to be examined and the relative amount of each subject to be covered, you can choose suitable study materials. For beginning level jobs, or even advanced ones, if you have a pronounced weakness in some aspect of your training, read a modern, standard textbook in that field. Be sure it is up to date and has general coverage. Such books are normally available at your library, and the librarian will be glad to help you locate one. For entry-level positions, questions of appropriate difficulty are chosen – neither highly advanced questions, nor those too simple. Such questions require careful thought but not advanced training.

If the position for which you are applying is technical or advanced, you will read more advanced, specialized material. If you are already familiar with the basic principles of your field, elementary textbooks would waste your time. Concentrate on advanced textbooks and technical periodicals. Think through the concepts and review difficult problems in your field.

These are all general sources. You can get more ideas on your own initiative, following these leads. For example, training manuals and publications of the government agency which employs workers in your field can be useful, particularly for technical and professional positions. A letter or visit to the government department involved may result in more specific study suggestions, and certainly will provide you with a more definite idea of the exact nature of the position you are seeking.

III. KINDS OF TESTS

Tests are used for purposes other than measuring knowledge and ability to perform specified duties. For some positions, it is equally important to test ability to make adjustments to new situations or to profit from training. In others, basic mental abilities not dependent on information are essential. Questions which test these things may not appear as pertinent to the duties of the position as those which test for knowledge and information. Yet they are often highly important parts of a fair examination. For very general questions, it is almost impossible to help you direct your study efforts. What we can do is to point out some of the more common of these general abilities needed in public service positions and describe some typical questions.

1) General information

Broad, general information has been found useful for predicting job success in some kinds of work. This is tested in a variety of ways, from vocabulary lists to questions about current events. Basic background in some field of work, such as sociology or economics, may be sampled in a group of questions. Often these are principles which have become familiar to most persons through exposure rather than through formal training. It is difficult to advise you how to study for these questions; being alert to the world around you is our best suggestion.

2) Verbal ability

An example of an ability needed in many positions is verbal or language ability. Verbal ability is, in brief, the ability to use and understand words. Vocabulary and grammar tests are typical measures of this ability. Reading comprehension or paragraph interpretation questions are common in many kinds of civil service tests. You are given a paragraph of written material and asked to find its central meaning.

3) Numerical ability

Number skills can be tested by the familiar arithmetic problem, by checking paired lists of numbers to see which are alike and which are different, or by interpreting charts and graphs. In the latter test, a graph may be printed in the test booklet which you are asked to use as the basis for answering questions.

4) Observation

A popular test for law-enforcement positions is the observation test. A picture is shown to you for several minutes, then taken away. Questions about the picture test your ability to observe both details and larger elements.

5) Following directions

In many positions in the public service, the employee must be able to carry out written instructions dependably and accurately. You may be given a chart with several columns, each column listing a variety of information. The questions require you to carry out directions involving the information given in the chart.

6) Skills and aptitudes

Performance tests effectively measure some manual skills and aptitudes. When the skill is one in which you are trained, such as typing or shorthand, you can practice. These tests are often very much like those given in business school or high school courses. For many of the other skills and aptitudes, however, no short-time preparation can be made. Skills and abilities natural to you or that you have developed throughout your lifetime are being tested.

Many of the general questions just described provide all the data needed to answer the questions and ask you to use your reasoning ability to find the answers. Your best preparation for these tests, as well as for tests of facts and ideas, is to be at your physical and mental best. You, no doubt, have your own methods of getting into an exam-taking mood and keeping "in shape." The next section lists some ideas on this subject.

IV. KINDS OF QUESTIONS

Only rarely is the "essay" question, which you answer in narrative form, used in civil service tests. Civil service tests are usually of the short-answer type. Full instructions for answering these questions will be given to you at the examination. But in case this is your first experience with short-answer questions and separate answer sheets, here is what you need to know:

1) Multiple-choice Questions

Most popular of the short-answer questions is the "multiple choice" or "best answer" question. It can be used, for example, to test for factual knowledge, ability to solve problems or judgment in meeting situations found at work.

A multiple-choice question is normally one of three types—

- It can begin with an incomplete statement followed by several possible endings. You are to find the one ending which *best* completes the statement, although some of the others may not be entirely wrong.
- It can also be a complete statement in the form of a question which is answered by choosing one of the statements listed.

- It can be in the form of a problem – again you select the best answer.

Here is an example of a multiple-choice question with a discussion which should give you some clues as to the method for choosing the right answer:

When an employee has a complaint about his assignment, the action which will *best* help him overcome his difficulty is to

A. discuss his difficulty with his coworkers
B. take the problem to the head of the organization
C. take the problem to the person who gave him the assignment
D. say nothing to anyone about his complaint

In answering this question, you should study each of the choices to find which is best. Consider choice "A" – Certainly an employee may discuss his complaint with fellow employees, but no change or improvement can result, and the complaint remains unresolved. Choice "B" is a poor choice since the head of the organization probably does not know what assignment you have been given, and taking your problem to him is known as "going over the head" of the supervisor. The supervisor, or person who made the assignment, is the person who can clarify it or correct any injustice. Choice "C" is, therefore, correct. To say nothing, as in choice "D," is unwise. Supervisors have and interest in knowing the problems employees are facing, and the employee is seeking a solution to his problem.

2) True/False Questions

The "true/false" or "right/wrong" form of question is sometimes used. Here a complete statement is given. Your job is to decide whether the statement is right or wrong.

SAMPLE: A roaming cell-phone call to a nearby city costs less than a non-roaming call to a distant city.

This statement is wrong, or false, since roaming calls are more expensive.

This is not a complete list of all possible question forms, although most of the others are variations of these common types. You will always get complete directions for answering questions. Be sure you understand *how* to mark your answers – ask questions until you do.

V. RECORDING YOUR ANSWERS

Computer terminals are used more and more today for many different kinds of exams.

For an examination with very few applicants, you may be told to record your answers in the test booklet itself. Separate answer sheets are much more common. If this separate answer sheet is to be scored by machine – and this is often the case – it is highly important that you mark your answers correctly in order to get credit.

An electronic scoring machine is often used in civil service offices because of the speed with which papers can be scored. Machine-scored answer sheets must be marked with a pencil, which will be given to you. This pencil has a high graphite content which responds to the electronic scoring machine. As a matter of fact, stray dots may register as answers, so do not let your pencil rest on the answer sheet while you are pondering the correct answer. Also, if your pencil lead breaks or is otherwise defective, ask for another.

Since the answer sheet will be dropped in a slot in the scoring machine, be careful not to bend the corners or get the paper crumpled.

The answer sheet normally has five vertical columns of numbers, with 30 numbers to a column. These numbers correspond to the question numbers in your test booklet. After each number, going across the page are four or five pairs of dotted lines. These short dotted lines have small letters or numbers above them. The first two pairs may also have a "T" or "F" above the letters. This indicates that the first two pairs only are to be used if the questions are of the true-false type. If the questions are multiple choice, disregard the "T" and "F" and pay attention only to the small letters or numbers.

Answer your questions in the manner of the sample that follows:

32. The largest city in the United States is
    A. Washington, D.C.
    B. New York City
    C. Chicago
    D. Detroit
    E. San Francisco

1) Choose the answer you think is best. (New York City is the largest, so "B" is correct.)
2) Find the row of dotted lines numbered the same as the question you are answering. (Find row number 32)
3) Find the pair of dotted lines corresponding to the answer. (Find the pair of lines under the mark "B.")
4) Make a solid black mark between the dotted lines.

VI. BEFORE THE TEST

Common sense will help you find procedures to follow to get ready for an examination. Too many of us, however, overlook these sensible measures. Indeed, nervousness and fatigue have been found to be the most serious reasons why applicants fail to do their best on civil service tests. Here is a list of reminders:

- Begin your preparation early – Don't wait until the last minute to go scurrying around for books and materials or to find out what the position is all about.
- Prepare continuously – An hour a night for a week is better than an all-night cram session. This has been definitely established. What is more, a night a week for a month will return better dividends than crowding your study into a shorter period of time.
- Locate the place of the exam – You have been sent a notice telling you when and where to report for the examination. If the location is in a different town or otherwise unfamiliar to you, it would be well to inquire the best route and learn something about the building.
- Relax the night before the test – Allow your mind to rest. Do not study at all that night. Plan some mild recreation or diversion; then go to bed early and get a good night's sleep.
- Get up early enough to make a leisurely trip to the place for the test – This way unforeseen events, traffic snarls, unfamiliar buildings, etc. will not upset you.
- Dress comfortably – A written test is not a fashion show. You will be known by number and not by name, so wear something comfortable.

- Leave excess paraphernalia at home – Shopping bags and odd bundles will get in your way. You need bring only the items mentioned in the official notice you received; usually everything you need is provided. Do not bring reference books to the exam. They will only confuse those last minutes and be taken away from you when in the test room.
- Arrive somewhat ahead of time – If because of transportation schedules you must get there very early, bring a newspaper or magazine to take your mind off yourself while waiting.
- Locate the examination room – When you have found the proper room, you will be directed to the seat or part of the room where you will sit. Sometimes you are given a sheet of instructions to read while you are waiting. Do not fill out any forms until you are told to do so; just read them and be prepared.
- Relax and prepare to listen to the instructions
- If you have any physical problem that may keep you from doing your best, be sure to tell the test administrator. If you are sick or in poor health, you really cannot do your best on the exam. You can come back and take the test some other time.

VII. AT THE TEST

The day of the test is here and you have the test booklet in your hand. The temptation to get going is very strong. Caution! There is more to success than knowing the right answers. You must know how to identify your papers and understand variations in the type of short-answer question used in this particular examination. Follow these suggestions for maximum results from your efforts:

1) Cooperate with the monitor

The test administrator has a duty to create a situation in which you can be as much at ease as possible. He will give instructions, tell you when to begin, check to see that you are marking your answer sheet correctly, and so on. He is not there to guard you, although he will see that your competitors do not take unfair advantage. He wants to help you do your best.

2) Listen to all instructions

Don't jump the gun! Wait until you understand all directions. In most civil service tests you get more time than you need to answer the questions. So don't be in a hurry. Read each word of instructions until you clearly understand the meaning. Study the examples, listen to all announcements and follow directions. Ask questions if you do not understand what to do.

3) Identify your papers

Civil service exams are usually identified by number only. You will be assigned a number; you must not put your name on your test papers. Be sure to copy your number correctly. Since more than one exam may be given, copy your exact examination title.

4) Plan your time

Unless you are told that a test is a "speed" or "rate of work" test, speed itself is usually not important. Time enough to answer all the questions will be provided, but this does not mean that you have all day. An overall time limit has been set. Divide the total time (in minutes) by the number of questions to determine the approximate time you have for each question.

5) Do not linger over difficult questions

If you come across a difficult question, mark it with a paper clip (useful to have along) and come back to it when you have been through the booklet. One caution if you do this – be sure to skip a number on your answer sheet as well. Check often to be sure that you have not lost your place and that you are marking in the row numbered the same as the question you are answering.

6) Read the questions

Be sure you know what the question asks! Many capable people are unsuccessful because they failed to *read* the questions correctly.

7) Answer all questions

Unless you have been instructed that a penalty will be deducted for incorrect answers, it is better to guess than to omit a question.

8) Speed tests

It is often better NOT to guess on speed tests. It has been found that on timed tests people are tempted to spend the last few seconds before time is called in marking answers at random – without even reading them – in the hope of picking up a few extra points. To discourage this practice, the instructions may warn you that your score will be "corrected" for guessing. That is, a penalty will be applied. The incorrect answers will be deducted from the correct ones, or some other penalty formula will be used.

9) Review your answers

If you finish before time is called, go back to the questions you guessed or omitted to give them further thought. Review other answers if you have time.

10) Return your test materials

If you are ready to leave before others have finished or time is called, take ALL your materials to the monitor and leave quietly. Never take any test material with you. The monitor can discover whose papers are not complete, and taking a test booklet may be grounds for disqualification.

VIII. EXAMINATION TECHNIQUES

1) Read the general instructions carefully. These are usually printed on the first page of the exam booklet. As a rule, these instructions refer to the timing of the examination; the fact that you should not start work until the signal and must stop work at a signal, etc. If there are any *special* instructions, such as a choice of questions to be answered, make sure that you note this instruction carefully.

2) When you are ready to start work on the examination, that is as soon as the signal has been given, read the instructions to each question booklet, underline any key words or phrases, such as *least, best, outline, describe* and the like. In this way you will tend to answer as requested rather than discover on reviewing your paper that you *listed without describing*, that you selected the *worst* choice rather than the *best* choice, etc.

3) If the examination is of the objective or multiple-choice type – that is, each question will also give a series of possible answers: A, B, C or D, and you are called upon to select the best answer and write the letter next to that answer on your answer paper – it is advisable to start answering each question in turn. There may be anywhere from 50 to 100 such questions in the three or four hours allotted and you can see how much time would be taken if you read through all the questions before beginning to answer any. Furthermore, if you come across a question or group of questions which you know would be difficult to answer, it would undoubtedly affect your handling of all the other questions.

4) If the examination is of the essay type and contains but a few questions, it is a moot point as to whether you should read all the questions before starting to answer any one. Of course, if you are given a choice – say five out of seven and the like – then it is essential to read all the questions so you can eliminate the two that are most difficult. If, however, you are asked to answer all the questions, there may be danger in trying to answer the easiest one first because you may find that you will spend too much time on it. The best technique is to answer the first question, then proceed to the second, etc.

5) Time your answers. Before the exam begins, write down the time it started, then add the time allowed for the examination and write down the time it must be completed, then divide the time available somewhat as follows:
   - If 3-1/2 hours are allowed, that would be 210 minutes. If you have 80 objective-type questions, that would be an average of 2-1/2 minutes per question. Allow yourself no more than 2 minutes per question, or a total of 160 minutes, which will permit about 50 minutes to review.
   - If for the time allotment of 210 minutes there are 7 essay questions to answer, that would average about 30 minutes a question. Give yourself only 25 minutes per question so that you have about 35 minutes to review.

6) The most important instruction is to *read each question* and make sure you know what is wanted. The second most important instruction is to *time yourself properly* so that you answer every question. The third most important instruction is to *answer every question*. Guess if you have to but include something for each question. Remember that you will receive no credit for a blank and will probably receive some credit if you write something in answer to an essay question. If you guess a letter – say "B" for a multiple-choice question – you may have guessed right. If you leave a blank as an answer to a multiple-choice question, the examiners may respect your feelings but it will not add a point to your score. Some exams may penalize you for wrong answers, so in such cases *only*, you may not want to guess unless you have some basis for your answer.

7) Suggestions
   a. Objective-type questions
      1. Examine the question booklet for proper sequence of pages and questions
      2. Read all instructions carefully
      3. Skip any question which seems too difficult; return to it after all other questions have been answered
      4. Apportion your time properly; do not spend too much time on any single question or group of questions

5. Note and underline key words – *all, most, fewest, least, best, worst, same, opposite,* etc.
6. Pay particular attention to negatives
7. Note unusual option, e.g., unduly long, short, complex, different or similar in content to the body of the question
8. Observe the use of "hedging" words – *probably, may, most likely,* etc.
9. Make sure that your answer is put next to the same number as the question
10. Do not second-guess unless you have good reason to believe the second answer is definitely more correct
11. Cross out original answer if you decide another answer is more accurate; do not erase until you are ready to hand your paper in
12. Answer all questions; guess unless instructed otherwise
13. Leave time for review

b. Essay questions
1. Read each question carefully
2. Determine exactly what is wanted. Underline key words or phrases.
3. Decide on outline or paragraph answer
4. Include many different points and elements unless asked to develop any one or two points or elements
5. Show impartiality by giving pros and cons unless directed to select one side only
6. Make and write down any assumptions you find necessary to answer the questions
7. Watch your English, grammar, punctuation and choice of words
8. Time your answers; don't crowd material

8) Answering the essay question

Most essay questions can be answered by framing the specific response around several key words or ideas. Here are a few such key words or ideas:

M's: manpower, materials, methods, money, management
P's: purpose, program, policy, plan, procedure, practice, problems, pitfalls, personnel, public relations

a. Six basic steps in handling problems:
1. Preliminary plan and background development
2. Collect information, data and facts
3. Analyze and interpret information, data and facts
4. Analyze and develop solutions as well as make recommendations
5. Prepare report and sell recommendations
6. Install recommendations and follow up effectiveness

b. Pitfalls to avoid
1. *Taking things for granted* – A statement of the situation does not necessarily imply that each of the elements is necessarily true; for example, a complaint may be invalid and biased so that all that can be taken for granted is that a complaint has been registered

2. *Considering only one side of a situation* – Wherever possible, indicate several alternatives and then point out the reasons you selected the best one
3. *Failing to indicate follow up* – Whenever your answer indicates action on your part, make certain that you will take proper follow-up action to see how successful your recommendations, procedures or actions turn out to be
4. *Taking too long in answering any single question* – Remember to time your answers properly

IX. AFTER THE TEST

Scoring procedures differ in detail among civil service jurisdictions although the general principles are the same. Whether the papers are hand-scored or graded by machine we have described, they are nearly always graded by number. That is, the person who marks the paper knows only the number – never the name – of the applicant. Not until all the papers have been graded will they be matched with names. If other tests, such as training and experience or oral interview ratings have been given, scores will be combined. Different parts of the examination usually have different weights. For example, the written test might count 60 percent of the final grade, and a rating of training and experience 40 percent. In many jurisdictions, veterans will have a certain number of points added to their grades.

After the final grade has been determined, the names are placed in grade order and an eligible list is established. There are various methods for resolving ties between those who get the same final grade – probably the most common is to place first the name of the person whose application was received first. Job offers are made from the eligible list in the order the names appear on it. You will be notified of your grade and your rank as soon as all these computations have been made. This will be done as rapidly as possible.

People who are found to meet the requirements in the announcement are called "eligibles." Their names are put on a list of eligible candidates. An eligible's chances of getting a job depend on how high he stands on this list and how fast agencies are filling jobs from the list.

When a job is to be filled from a list of eligibles, the agency asks for the names of people on the list of eligibles for that job. When the civil service commission receives this request, it sends to the agency the names of the three people highest on this list. Or, if the job to be filled has specialized requirements, the office sends the agency the names of the top three persons who meet these requirements from the general list.

The appointing officer makes a choice from among the three people whose names were sent to him. If the selected person accepts the appointment, the names of the others are put back on the list to be considered for future openings.

That is the rule in hiring from all kinds of eligible lists, whether they are for typist, carpenter, chemist, or something else. For every vacancy, the appointing officer has his choice of any one of the top three eligibles on the list. This explains why the person whose name is on top of the list sometimes does not get an appointment when some of the persons lower on the list do. If the appointing officer chooses the second or third eligible, the No. 1 eligible does not get a job at once, but stays on the list until he is appointed or the list is terminated.

X. HOW TO PASS THE INTERVIEW TEST

The examination for which you applied requires an oral interview test. You have already taken the written test and you are now being called for the interview test – the final part of the formal examination.

You may think that it is not possible to prepare for an interview test and that there are no procedures to follow during an interview. Our purpose is to point out some things you can do in advance that will help you and some good rules to follow and pitfalls to avoid while you are being interviewed.

What is an interview supposed to test?

The written examination is designed to test the technical knowledge and competence of the candidate; the oral is designed to evaluate intangible qualities, not readily measured otherwise, and to establish a list showing the relative fitness of each candidate – as measured against his competitors – for the position sought. Scoring is not on the basis of "right" and "wrong," but on a sliding scale of values ranging from "not passable" to "outstanding." As a matter of fact, it is possible to achieve a relatively low score without a single "incorrect" answer because of evident weakness in the qualities being measured.

Occasionally, an examination may consist entirely of an oral test – either an individual or a group oral. In such cases, information is sought concerning the technical knowledges and abilities of the candidate, since there has been no written examination for this purpose. More commonly, however, an oral test is used to supplement a written examination.

Who conducts interviews?

The composition of oral boards varies among different jurisdictions. In nearly all, a representative of the personnel department serves as chairman. One of the members of the board may be a representative of the department in which the candidate would work. In some cases, "outside experts" are used, and, frequently, a businessman or some other representative of the general public is asked to serve. Labor and management or other special groups may be represented. The aim is to secure the services of experts in the appropriate field.

However the board is composed, it is a good idea (and not at all improper or unethical) to ascertain in advance of the interview who the members are and what groups they represent. When you are introduced to them, you will have some idea of their backgrounds and interests, and at least you will not stutter and stammer over their names.

What should be done before the interview?

While knowledge about the board members is useful and takes some of the surprise element out of the interview, there is other preparation which is more substantive. It *is* possible to prepare for an oral interview – in several ways:

1) Keep a copy of your application and review it carefully before the interview

This may be the only document before the oral board, and the starting point of the interview. Know what education and experience you have listed there, and the sequence and dates of all of it. Sometimes the board will ask you to review the highlights of your experience for them; you should not have to hem and haw doing it.

2) Study the class specification and the examination announcement

Usually, the oral board has one or both of these to guide them. The qualities, characteristics or knowledges required by the position sought are stated in these documents. They offer valuable clues as to the nature of the oral interview. For example, if the job involves supervisory responsibilities, the announcement will usually indicate that knowledge of modern supervisory methods and the qualifications of the candidate as a supervisor will be tested. If so, you can expect such questions, frequently in the form of a hypothetical situation which you are expected to solve. NEVER go into an oral without knowledge of the duties and responsibilities of the job you seek.

3) Think through each qualification required

Try to visualize the kind of questions you would ask if you were a board member. How well could you answer them? Try especially to appraise your own knowledge and background in each area, *measured against the job sought*, and identify any areas in which you are weak. Be critical and realistic – do not flatter yourself.

4) Do some general reading in areas in which you feel you may be weak

For example, if the job involves supervision and your past experience has NOT, some general reading in supervisory methods and practices, particularly in the field of human relations, might be useful. Do NOT study agency procedures or detailed manuals. The oral board will be testing your understanding and capacity, not your memory.

5) Get a good night's sleep and watch your general health and mental attitude

You will want a clear head at the interview. Take care of a cold or any other minor ailment, and of course, no hangovers.

What should be done on the day of the interview?

Now comes the day of the interview itself. Give yourself plenty of time to get there. Plan to arrive somewhat ahead of the scheduled time, particularly if your appointment is in the fore part of the day. If a previous candidate fails to appear, the board might be ready for you a bit early. By early afternoon an oral board is almost invariably behind schedule if there are many candidates, and you may have to wait. Take along a book or magazine to read, or your application to review, but leave any extraneous material in the waiting room when you go in for your interview. In any event, relax and compose yourself.

The matter of dress is important. The board is forming impressions about you – from your experience, your manners, your attitude, and your appearance. Give your personal appearance careful attention. Dress your best, but not your flashiest. Choose conservative, appropriate clothing, and be sure it is immaculate. This is a business interview, and your appearance should indicate that you regard it as such. Besides, being well groomed and properly dressed will help boost your confidence.

Sooner or later, someone will call your name and escort you into the interview room. *This is it.* From here on you are on your own. It is too late for any more preparation. But remember, you asked for this opportunity to prove your fitness, and you are here because your request was granted.

What happens when you go in?

The usual sequence of events will be as follows: The clerk (who is often the board stenographer) will introduce you to the chairman of the oral board, who will introduce you to the other members of the board. Acknowledge the introductions before you sit down. Do not be surprised if you find a microphone facing you or a stenotypist sitting by. Oral interviews are usually recorded in the event of an appeal or other review.

Usually the chairman of the board will open the interview by reviewing the highlights of your education and work experience from your application – primarily for the benefit of the other members of the board, as well as to get the material into the record. Do not interrupt or comment unless there is an error or significant misinterpretation; if that is the case, do not hesitate. But do not quibble about insignificant matters. Also, he will usually ask you some question about your education, experience or your present job – partly to get you to start talking and to establish the interviewing "rapport." He may start the actual questioning, or turn it over to one of the other members. Frequently, each member undertakes the questioning on a particular area, one in which he is perhaps most competent, so you can expect each member to participate in the examination. Because time is limited, you may also expect some rather abrupt switches in the direction the questioning takes, so do not be upset by it. Normally, a board member will not pursue a single line of questioning unless he discovers a particular strength or weakness.

After each member has participated, the chairman will usually ask whether any member has any further questions, then will ask you if you have anything you wish to add. Unless you are expecting this question, it may floor you. Worse, it may start you off on an extended, extemporaneous speech. The board is not usually seeking more information. The question is principally to offer you a last opportunity to present further qualifications or to indicate that you have nothing to add. So, if you feel that a significant qualification or characteristic has been overlooked, it is proper to point it out in a sentence or so. Do not compliment the board on the thoroughness of their examination – they have been sketchy, and you know it. If you wish, merely say, "No thank you, I have nothing further to add." This is a point where you can "talk yourself out" of a good impression or fail to present an important bit of information. Remember, *you close the interview yourself.*

The chairman will then say, "That is all, Mr. ______, thank you." Do not be startled; the interview is over, and quicker than you think. Thank him, gather your belongings and take your leave. Save your sigh of relief for the other side of the door.

How to put your best foot forward

Throughout this entire process, you may feel that the board individually and collectively is trying to pierce your defenses, seek out your hidden weaknesses and embarrass and confuse you. Actually, this is not true. They are obliged to make an appraisal of your qualifications for the job you are seeking, and they want to see you in your best light. Remember, they must interview all candidates and a non-cooperative candidate may become a failure in spite of their best efforts to bring out his qualifications. Here are 15 suggestions that will help you:

1) Be natural – Keep your attitude confident, not cocky

If you are not confident that you can do the job, do not expect the board to be. Do not apologize for your weaknesses, try to bring out your strong points. The board is interested in a positive, not negative, presentation. Cockiness will antagonize any board member and make him wonder if you are covering up a weakness by a false show of strength.

2) Get comfortable, but don't lounge or sprawl

Sit erectly but not stiffly. A careless posture may lead the board to conclude that you are careless in other things, or at least that you are not impressed by the importance of the occasion. Either conclusion is natural, even if incorrect. Do not fuss with your clothing, a pencil or an ashtray. Your hands may occasionally be useful to emphasize a point; do not let them become a point of distraction.

3) Do not wisecrack or make small talk

This is a serious situation, and your attitude should show that you consider it as such. Further, the time of the board is limited – they do not want to waste it, and neither should you.

4) Do not exaggerate your experience or abilities

In the first place, from information in the application or other interviews and sources, the board may know more about you than you think. Secondly, you probably will not get away with it. An experienced board is rather adept at spotting such a situation, so do not take the chance.

5) If you know a board member, do not make a point of it, yet do not hide it

Certainly you are not fooling him, and probably not the other members of the board. Do not try to take advantage of your acquaintanceship – it will probably do you little good.

6) Do not dominate the interview

Let the board do that. They will give you the clues – do not assume that you have to do all the talking. Realize that the board has a number of questions to ask you, and do not try to take up all the interview time by showing off your extensive knowledge of the answer to the first one.

7) Be attentive

You only have 20 minutes or so, and you should keep your attention at its sharpest throughout. When a member is addressing a problem or question to you, give him your undivided attention. Address your reply principally to him, but do not exclude the other board members.

8) Do not interrupt

A board member may be stating a problem for you to analyze. He will ask you a question when the time comes. Let him state the problem, and wait for the question.

9) Make sure you understand the question

Do not try to answer until you are sure what the question is. If it is not clear, restate it in your own words or ask the board member to clarify it for you. However, do not haggle about minor elements.

10) Reply promptly but not hastily

A common entry on oral board rating sheets is "candidate responded readily," or "candidate hesitated in replies." Respond as promptly and quickly as you can, but do not jump to a hasty, ill-considered answer.

11) Do not be peremptory in your answers

A brief answer is proper – but do not fire your answer back. That is a losing game from your point of view. The board member can probably ask questions much faster than you can answer them.

12) Do not try to create the answer you think the board member wants

He is interested in what kind of mind you have and how it works – not in playing games. Furthermore, he can usually spot this practice and will actually grade you down on it.

13) Do not switch sides in your reply merely to agree with a board member

Frequently, a member will take a contrary position merely to draw you out and to see if you are willing and able to defend your point of view. Do not start a debate, yet do not surrender a good position. If a position is worth taking, it is worth defending.

14) Do not be afraid to admit an error in judgment if you are shown to be wrong

The board knows that you are forced to reply without any opportunity for careful consideration. Your answer may be demonstrably wrong. If so, admit it and get on with the interview.

15) Do not dwell at length on your present job

The opening question may relate to your present assignment. Answer the question but do not go into an extended discussion. You are being examined for a *new* job, not your present one. As a matter of fact, try to phrase ALL your answers in terms of the job for which you are being examined.

Basis of Rating

Probably you will forget most of these "do's" and "don'ts" when you walk into the oral interview room. Even remembering them all will not ensure you a passing grade. Perhaps you did not have the qualifications in the first place. But remembering them will help you to put your best foot forward, without treading on the toes of the board members.

Rumor and popular opinion to the contrary notwithstanding, an oral board wants you to make the best appearance possible. They know you are under pressure – but they also want to see how you respond to it as a guide to what your reaction would be under the pressures of the job you seek. They will be influenced by the degree of poise you display, the personal traits you show and the manner in which you respond.

ABOUT THIS BOOK

This book contains tests divided into Examination Sections. Go through each test, answering every question in the margin. We have also attached a sample answer sheet at the back of the book that can be removed and used. At the end of each test look at the answer key and check your answers. On the ones you got wrong, look at the right answer choice and learn. Do not fill in the answers first. Do not memorize the questions and answers, but understand the answer and principles involved. On your test, the questions will likely be different from the samples. Questions are changed and new ones added. If you understand these past questions you should have success with any changes that arise. Tests may consist of several types of questions. We have additional books on each subject should more study be advisable or necessary for you. Finally, the more you study, the better prepared you will be. This book is intended to be the last thing you study before you walk into the examination room. Prior study of relevant texts is also recommended. NLC publishes some of these in our Fundamental Series. Knowledge and good sense are important factors in passing your exam. Good luck also helps. So now study this Passbook, absorb the material contained within and take that knowledge into the examination. Then do your best to pass that exam.

EXAMINATION SECTION

EXAMINATION SECTION
TEST 1

DIRECTIONS: Each question or incomplete statement is followed by several suggested answers or completions. Select the one that BEST answers the question or completes the statement. *PRINT THE LETTER OF THE CORRECT ANSWER IN THE SPACE AT THE RIGHT.*

1. Of the following, the MOST efficient way to handle and store heavy objects loaded on pallets in a warehouse is with the aid of a 1.____

   A. conveyor belt
   B. hand truck
   C. dolly
   D. forklift

2. You receive 20 large glass containers of highly dangerous acid. Of the following, it would be SAFEST to store these glass containers in ______ area. 2.____

   A. a special designated
   B. a busy workshop
   C. the main storage
   D. the shipping and receiving

Questions 3-7.

DIRECTIONS: Questions 3 through 7 each contains a description of a stock item which is incomplete. You are to answer each question by selecting the term which BEST completes the description of the item.

EXAMPLE: Brush, tooth, adult size
A. nylon bristle
B. glass handle
C. 18 inches
D. fluoride

The CORRECT answer is A, which completes the description of a toothbrush.

3. Polish, furniture, one quart can 3.____

   A. gasoline
   B. acid
   C. lemon oil
   D. glue substance

4. Card, index, ruled, white 4.____

   A. bond B. 3" x 5" C. round D. plastic

5. Sugar, 1/6 ounce, individual package 5.____

   A. soft B. mixed C. sprinkled D. granulated

6. Pad, gauze, 2 in. x 2 in. 6.____

   A. sterile B. paper C. rubber D. cold

7. Shovel, snow, square point 7.____

   A. sweeper B. duster C. long handle D. saw tooth

8. There are times when birds find their way into a warehouse and make nests. This may cause problems to the store-keeping operations.
Of the following, the MOST practical way to deal with this matter is to ______ the warehouse. 8.___

   A. place bird feed outside
   B. plant trees around
   C. provide bird perches in
   D. destroy bird nests in

9. Entries of incoming and outgoing stock items are made on individual stock cards for all the following reasons EXCEPT 9.___

   A. detecting possible stealing of the stock items
   B. keeping an accurate record of the stock items
   C. officially recording the entries of incoming and outgoing stock items
   D. showing your supervisor what a good job you can do

10. A particular stock item presently shows an inventory balance smaller than the inventory balance of the previous month.
Of the following, this information shows you that the quantity of this particular item 10.___

   A. issued was more than the amount received
   B. issued was less than the amount received
   C. received was equal to the amount issued
   D. received was more than the amount issued

Questions 11-12.

DIRECTIONS: Questions 11 and 12 are to be answered on the basis of the information given in the following passage relating to an Executive Order by the Mayor.

The Commissioner of Investigation shall have general responsibility for the investigation and elimination of corrupt or other criminal activity, conflicts of interest, unethical conduct, misconduct, and incompetence by city agencies, by city officers and employees, and by persons regulated by, doing business with, or receiving funds directly or indirectly from the city, with respect to their dealings with the city. All agency heads shall be responsible for establishing, subject to review for completeness and inter-agency consistency by the Commissioner of Investigation, written standards of conduct for the officials and employees of their respective agencies, and fair and efficient disciplinary systems to maintain those standards of conduct. All agencies shall have an Inspector General who shall report directly to the respective agency head and to the Commissioner of Investigation and be responsible for maintaining standards of conduct as may be established in such agency under this Order. Inspectors General shall be responsible for the investigation and elimination of corrupt or other criminal activity, conflicts of interest, unethical conduct, misconduct and incompetence within their respective agencies. Except to the extent otherwise provided by law, the employment or continued employment of all existing and prospective Inspectors General and members of their staffs shall be subject to complete background investigations and approval by the Department of Investigation.

11. According to the above passage, establishing written standards of conduct for each agency is the responsibility of the 11.____

A. agency head
B. Commissioner of Investigation
C. Department of Investigation
D. Inspector General

12. According to the above passage, maintaining standards of conduct within each agency is the responsibility of the 12.____

A. agency head
B. Commissioner of Investigation
C. Department of Investigation
D. Inspector General

Questions 13-16.

DIRECTIONS: Questions 13 through 16 are to be answered on the basis of the following information.

Assume that Warehouse X uses the following procedures for receiving stock. When a delivery is received, the stock handler who receives the delivery should immediately unpack and check the delivery. This check is to ensure that the quantity and kinds of stock items delivered match those on the purchase order which had been sent to the vendor. After the delivery is checked, a receiving report is prepared by the same stock handler. This receiving report should include the name of the shipper, the purchase order number, the description of the item, and the actual count or weight of the item. The receiving report, along with the packing slip, should then be checked by the stores clerk against the purchase order to make sure that the quantity received is correct. This is necessary before credit can be obtained from the vendor for any items that are missing or damaged. After the checking is completed, the stock items can be moved to the stockroom.

13. According to the procedures described above, the stock person who receives the delivery should 13.____

A. placed the unopened delivery in a secure area for checking at a later date
B. notify the stores clerk that the delivery has arrived and is ready for checking
C. unpack the delivery and check the quantity and types of stock items against the purchase order
D. closely examine the outside of the delivery containers for dents and damages

14. According to the procedures described above, credit can be obtained from the vendor 14.____

A. *before* the stock handler checks the delivery of stock items
B. *after* the stock handler checks the delivery of stock items
C. *before* the stores clerk checks the receiving report against the purchase order
D. *after* the stores clerk checks the receiving report against the purchase order

15. According to the procedures described above, all of the following information should be included when filling out a receiving report EXCEPT the 15.____

A. purchase order number
B. name of the shipper
C. count or weight of the item
D. unit cost per item

16. According to the procedures described above, after the stores clerk has checked the receiving report against the purchase order, the NEXT step is to 16.____

A. move the stock items to the stockroom
B. return the stock items received to the vendor
C. give the stock items to the stock handler for final checking
D. file the packing slip for inventory purposes

17. All of the following would be good ways for you to show an employee how to pack a box EXCEPT 17.____

A. making sure that the employee can clearly see what you are doing
B. going through the process slowly and carefully with the employee
C. talking and working as quickly as you can, so that you don't bore the employee
D. explaining the purpose of each step to the employee

18. You are starting to prepare a requisition for certain supplies, which must be done as soon as possible. A co-worker comes to you and asks you for your help in finding several stock items. You are told that finding these items will take some time. You decide to finish preparing the requisition first before you help your co-worker. 18.____
Of the following, your action can BEST be described as

A. *acceptable* because you must prepare the requisition as quickly as possible
B. *unacceptable* because you should help your co-worker
C. *acceptable* because your co-worker should be able to do the job alone
D. *unacceptable* because you can finish preparing the requisition some other time

19. A newly-hired employee has just been assigned to work under your supervision. You want to be sure that the employee will do the job well and perform it properly. Of the following, the FIRST action you should take is to 19.____

A. tell the employee exactly what has to be done and what is expected
B. allow the employee to begin work on a difficult task immediately
C. assign the employee to work with others who have little experience
D. give the employee enough work to keep busy

20. You observe two of your subordinates, Mr. White and Mr. Wilson, lifting heavy items together. You see that Mr. White is not lifting the items properly while Mr. Wilson is. As the supervisor, the MOST appropriate action for you to take in this situation is to 20.____

A. allow Mr. White time to learn by himself the correct way to lift heavy items
B. have Mr. Wilson lift the heavy items by himself
C. show Mr. White how to lift the heavy items properly
D. advise Mr. Wilson to be very careful when working with Mr. White

21. One of your subordinates asks you to meet with him privately to discuss a personal problem which he feels is affecting his work performance. You know that you have a very busy work schedule every day. 21.____
As the supervisor, the BEST way for you to handle this situation is to

A. tell the subordinate that you are too busy to meet with him today but to try again in a few days
B. tell the subordinate that it is not proper to discuss personal problems
C. schedule a meeting with the subordinate for that same day
D. tell the subordinate that you will hold a group meeting soon to discuss any problems

22. One of your responsibilities as a supervisor is to make sure that the unit area is cleaned up each day. You know that no one in your unit likes to do the cleaning. In order to minimize any dissatisfaction on the part of your subordinates, it would be BEST for you to assign this work 22.____

A. to the strongest worker in your unit
B. on a rotating basis
C. to the slowest worker in your unit
D. on a disciplinary basis

23. Two of your subordinates approach you and ask you to help them with a disagreement they are having about their job duties. 23.____
The BEST approach for you to take in dealing with this situation is to

A. tell the subordinates they should be able to settle the disagreement themselves
B. check with other subordinates to find out if they can be of any help
C. tell the subordinates to return to work and not to discuss the matter any further
D. listen to what each subordinate has to say and then try to help them to reach an agreement

24. Assume that food items, as they are received, are clearly dated on the outside of each package by the receiver. 24.____
If you assign one of your subordinates to pick the oldest stock of food items first when filling an order, then you should expect the subordinate to find the oldest stock by

A. checking the date on the outside of each package
B. opening each package and checking the items inside
C. getting the information from the receiver
D. asking you for the information

25. One of your subordinates has been arriving at work about one-half hour late every day for the past two weeks. However, the subordinate is able to complete the work on time and continues to do a good job. 25.____
As the supervisor, the BEST way for you to deal with this matter is to

A. talk to the subordinate in private about the lateness
B. praise the subordinate for the good work being done
C. say nothing because the subordinate is still doing the job well
D. ask your superior what you should do

26. Assume that you have outlined four steps you are going to take in solving a storekeeping problem. These steps are as follows: 26.____

I. Analyze the facts.
II. Define the problem.
III. List possible solutions.
IV. Get the facts.

Which one of the following shows the order of taking these steps that would be MOST effective in solving a problem?

A. IV, II, I, III
B. II, IV, I, III
C. III, I, II, IV
D. I, III, II, IV

Questions 27-31.

DIRECTIONS: Questions 27 through 31 are to be answered on the basis of the information given in Tables 1 and 2 of the DAILY PRODUCTIVITY REPORT shown below.

DAILY PRODUCTIVITY REPORT

Table 1

Standards	Unsatisfactory	Conditional	Satisfactory	Superior	Outstanding
Number of pieces packed per day	245 and below	246 to 289	290 to 347	348 to 405	406 and above

Table 2

Initials of the Packer	A.S	S.B.	B.D	L.M.	J.C	R.N.	B.G	C.A	D.F	E.R
Number of Pieces Packed Per Day	252	335	276	342	409	290	235	309	246	425

27. The number of packers whose productivity is *Outstanding* is 27.____

A. 4
B. 3
C. 2
D. 1

28. The number of packers who come under the *Conditional* productivity standard is 28.____

A. 1
B. 2
C. 3
D. 4

29. The percentage of packers whose productivity can be rated *Satisfactory* or higher is 29.____

A. 30%
B. 40%
C. 50%
D. 60%

30. If every packer's daily productivity increased by 20 pieces, the number of packers whose productivity ratings would change to the NEXT standard is 30.____

A. 4
B. 5
C. 6
D. 7

31. Which one of the following is an accurate statement that can be made based on the information shown in Tables 1 and 2? 31.____

A. There are more packers whose productivity is above the maximum *Satisfactory* level than below the minimum *Satisfactory* level.
B. There are more packers whose productivity is in the *Satisfactory* standard than in any one of the other four standards.
C. The number of packers whose productivity is *Unsatisfactory* is equal to the number of packers whose productivity is *Outstanding.*
D. There is at least one packer whose productivity is in each of the five standards.

Questions 32-35.

DIRECTIONS: Questions 32 through 35 are to be answered on the basis of the information given in the inventory tables shown below. Table 1 shows the amount of each item in stock according to the information contained on the perpetual inventory card for that item. Table 2 shows the amount of the same item in stock according to an inventory just completed by the staff.

Table 1

Perpetual Inventory Card	
Item No.	Amount of Stock
A107	2,564
A257	10,365
A342	7,018
A475	52,475
B026	16,207
B422	4,520
B717	21,431
B802	308
C328	594
C329	164
C438	723
C527	844

Table 2

Inventory Just Completed By Staff	
Item No.	Amount of Stock
A107	2,545
A257	10,356
A342	7,018
A475	52,475
B026	16,207
B422	4,505
B717	21,413
B802	308
C328	594
C329	143
C438	723
C527	854

32. In which one of the following items is there a difference between the amount of stock shown on the perpetual inventory card and in the inventory just completed? 32.____
Item No.

A. A257 B. B026 C. C328 D. C438

33. In which one of the following items is the difference GREATEST between the amount of stock shown on the perpetual inventory card and in the inventory just completed? 33.____
Item No.

A. A107 B. B422 C. B717 D. C329

34. The amount of stock shown for Item No. C527 on the inventory taken by the staff is greater than the amount shown on the perpetual inventory card. 34.____
Of the following, the LEAST likely reason for this difference is that the

A. perpetual inventory card was not brought up to date
B. staff did not take an accurate inventory
C. information entered on the perpetual inventory card was inaccurate
D. staff made an inventory on the wrong item

35. Which one of the following is an ACCURATE statement that can be made based on the information shown in Tables 1 and 2? 35.____

A. More than half of the items listed show a difference between the amount of stock shown on the perpetual inventory card and in the inventory just completed.
B. One-third of the items listed show the amount of stock on the perpetual inventory card and in the inventory just completed to be 10,000 or more.
C. Less than half of the items listed show a difference between the amount of stock shown on the perpetual inventory card and in the inventory just completed.
D. One-third of the items listed show the amount of stock on the perpetual inventory card and in the inventory just completed to be 10,000 or less.

36. You are preparing to hold a training session for your unit on the safe use of storekeeping equipment. 36.____
Of the following, the MOST important reason for you to give this training is to

A. answer any questions your workers may have about the use of the equipment
B. speed up the work done by the unit
C. reduce the amount of time lost for equipment repair
D. prevent accidents from happening when the equipment is being used

37. Of the following, the use of an *A* frame storage rack is MOST appropriate for storing 37.____

A. pipes or tubular items
B. crated goods
C. office supplies and equipment
D. empty pallets

38. Your warehouse is infested by rats. You have asked one of your subordinates to place rat traps throughout the warehouse in order to take care of the problem. 38.____
Of the following, the BEST way to use traps effectively is to

A. keep the same bait in the traps at all times
B. change the location of the traps frequently
C. disinfect the unused traps daily
D. place the traps in the busiest work areas

39. Of the following, the BEST way to determine how much of a certain item should be ordered each month is to 39.____

A. call the vendor of a similar item to find out how often that item is delivered to your agency
B. call another agency to find out how often deliveries of that item are made to that agency

C. keep an ongoing record of how much of the item is used during each month
D. increase the usual order so that your agency will never run out of that item

40. According to the information on a computer run, your stock of distilled water is short by 20 gallons. Of the following, the FIRST appropriate action you should take is to 40.____

A. check your own records of all the deliveries and issuances
B. let the computer unit know of their mistake
C. balance the shortage by showing an issuance of 20 gallons in the next report
D. buy 20 gallons of distilled water to make up the shortage

KEY (CORRECT ANSWERS)

1. D	11. A	21. C	31. B
2. A	12. D	22. B	32. A
3. C	13. C	23. D	33. D
4. B	14. D	24. A	34. D
5. D	15. D	25. A	35. B
6. A	16. A	26. B	36. D
7. C	17. C	27. C	37. A
8. D	18. A	28. C	38. B
9. D	19. A	29. D	39. C
10. A	20. C	30. A	40. A

TEST 2

DIRECTIONS: Each question or incomplete statement is followed by several suggested answers or completions. Select the one that BEST answers the question or completes the statement. *PRINT THE LETTER OF THE CORRECT ANSWER IN THE SPACE AT THE RIGHT.*

Questions 1-3.

DIRECTIONS: Questions 1 through 3 are to be answered on the basis of the information given in the passage below.

A filing system for requisition forms used in a warehouse will be of maximum benefit only if it provides ready access to information needed and is not too complex. How effective the system will be depends largely on how well the filing system is organized. A well-organized system usually results in a smooth-running operation.

When setting up a system for filing requisition forms, one effective method would be to first make an alphabetical listing of all the authorized requisitioning agencies. Then file folders should be prepared for each of these agencies and arranged alphabetically in file cabinets. Following this, each agency should be assigned a series of numbers corresponding to those on the blank requisition forms with which they will be supplied. When an agency then submits a requisition and it is filled, the form should be filed in numerical order in the designated agency folder. By using this system, any individual requisition form which is missing from its folder can be easily detected. Regardless of the filing system used, simplicity is essential if the filing system is to be successful.

1. According to the above passage, a filing system is MOST likely to be successful if it is 1.____

   A. alphabetical
   B. uncomplicated
   C. numerical
   D. reliable

2. According to the above passage, the reason numbers are assigned to each agency is to 2.____

   A. simplify stock issuing procedures
   B. keep a count of all incoming requisition forms
   C. be able to know when a form is missing from its folder
   D. eliminate the need for an alphabetical filing system

3. According to the above passage, which one of the following is an ACCURATE statement regarding the establishment of a well-organized filing system? 3.____

   A. Requisitioned stock items will be issued at a faster rate.
   B. Stock items will be stored in storage areas alphabetically arranged.
   C. Information concerning ordered stock items will be easily obtainable.
   D. Maximum productivity can be expected from each employee.

Questions 4-6.

DIRECTIONS: Questions 4 through 6 are to be answered on the basis of the information given in the chart below.

ITEM NUMBER TOTALS AS OF JANUARY 31

Item Number	Monthly Usage	Current Inventory	Time Required Between Ordering & Delivery of Item
1	460	1,000	1 month
2	475	1,500	2 months
3	225	1,500	4 months
4	500	2,500	5 months
5	1,150	1,950	2 months
6	775	4,700	5 months
7	850	1,700	2 months
8	900	3,600	3 months
9	175	525	2 months
10	1,325	5,300	3 months
11	225	900	4 months
12	425	1,500	1 month

4. Which one of the following, if not ordered by February 1, would cause the monthly usage to exceed the current inventory before new merchandise could be received? Item Number 4.____

A. 1 B. 4 C. 6 D. 10

5. Which one of the following must be ordered immediately because the current inventory cannot cover the monthly usage? Item Number 5.____

A. 2 B. 3 C. 5 D. 12

6. The date by which Item Numbers 8, 9, and 10 must be ordered so that the monthly usage does NOT exceed the current inventory is ______ . 6.____

A. February 1 B. March 1
C. April 1 D. May 1

7. When reviewing the monthly management report given to you by the supervisors of the units for which you are responsible, you find that one of the units has a large backlog of unfilled requisitions. 7.____
Of the following, the FIRST appropriate action you should take in handling this matter is to

A. order more stock of all the items stored in your warehouse
B. check with the supervisors of the other units and see how they would handle the matter
C. immediately hire more workers to take care of the backlog
D. consult with the supervisor of the unit which has the backlog to try to find the reason for it

8. You are assigning one of your subordinates, Mr. Jones, to do a task that he has never done before. It is important that he learn how to perform this task as soon as possible, but you do not have the time to train him. You decide to have a highly qualified subordinate, Mr. Smith, show him what must be done. 8.____
Of the following, your action concerning this situation can BEST be described as

A. *acceptable* because it is appropriate for a supervisor to delegate work to a capable subordinate
B. *unacceptable* because the training must be done by you, the supervisor
C. *acceptable* because Mr. Smith can do a better job of training Mr. Jones than you can
D. *unacceptable* because Mr. Smith will not be able to finish his regular duties

9. Jim Johnson has been on your staff for over four years. He has always been a conscientious and productive worker. About a month ago, his wife died; and since that time, his work performance has been very poor. 9.____
As his supervisor, which one of the following is the BEST way for you to deal with this situation?

A. Allow Jim as much time as he needs to overcome his grief and hope that his work performance improves.
B. Meet with Jim to discuss ways to improve his performance.
C. Tell Jim directly that you are more concerned with his work performance than with his personal problem.
D. Prepare disciplinary action on Jim as soon as possible.

10. You are responsible for the overall operation of a storehouse which is divided into two sections. Each section has its own supervisor. You have decided to make several complex changes in the storekeeping procedures which will affect both sections. 10.____
Of the following, the BEST way to make sure that these changes are understood by the two supervisors is for you to

A. meet with both supervisors to discuss the changes
B. issue a memorandum to each supervisor explaining the changes
C. post the changes where the supervisors are sure to see them
D. instruct one supervisor to explain the changes to the other supervisor

11. You have called a meeting of all your subordinates to tell them what has to be done on a new project in which they will all be involved. Several times during the meeting, you ask if there are any questions about what you have told them. 11.____
Of the following, to ask the subordinates whether there are any questions during the meeting can BEST be described as

A. *inadvisable* because it interferes with their learning about the new project
B. *advisable* because you will find out what they don't understand and have a chance to clear up any problems they may have
C. *inadvisable* because it makes the meeting too long and causes the subordinates to lose interest in the new project
D. *advisable* because it gives you a chance to learn which of your subordinates are paying attention to what you say

12. As a supervisor, you are responsible for seeing to it that absenteeism does not become a problem among your subordinates. 12.____
Which one of the following is NOT an acceptable way of controlling the problem of excessive absences?

A. Distribute a written statement to your staff on the policies regarding absenteeism in your organization.
B. Arrange for workers who have the fewest absences to talk to those workers who have the most absences.
C. Let your subordinates know that a record is being kept of all absences.
D. Arrange for counseling of those employees who are frequently absent.

13. One of your supervisors has been an excellent worker for the past two years. There are no promotion opportunities for this worker in the forseeable future. Due to the city's present budget crisis, a salary increase is not possible. 13.____
Under the circumstances, which one of the following actions on your part would be MOST likely to continue to motivate this worker?

A. Tell the worker that times are bad all over and jobs are hard to find.
B. Give the worker less work and easier assignments.
C. Tell the worker to try to look for a better paying job elsewhere.
D. Seek the worker's advice often and show that the suggestions provided are appreciated.

14. As a supervisor in a warehouse, it is important that you use your available work force to its fullest potential. Which one of the following actions on your part is MOST likely to increase the effectiveness of your work force? 14.____

A. Assigning more workers to a job than the number actually needed.
B. Eliminating all job training to allow more time for work output.
C. Using your best workers on jobs that average workers can do.
D. Making sure that all materials and equipment used are maintained in good working order.

15. You learn that your storage area will soon be undergoing changes which will affect the work of your subordinates. You decide not to tell your subordinates about what is to happen. 15.____
Of the following, your action can BEST be described as

A. *wise* because your subordinates will learn of the changes for themselves
B. *unwise* because your subordinates should be advised about what is to happen
C. *wise* because it is better for your subordinates to continue working without being disturbed by such news
D. *unwise* because the work of your subordinates will gradually slow down

16. In making plans for the operation of your unit, you are MOST likely to see these plans carried out successfully if you 16.____

A. allow your staff to participate in developing these plans
B. do not spend any time on the minor details of these plans
C. base these plans on the past experiences of others
D. allow these plans to interact with outside activities in other units

17. A colorless, odorless, and toxic gas that is contained in the exhausts of almost all internal combustion engines is 17.____

A. nitrogen
B. oxygen
C. carbon monoxide
D. sulphur dioxide

18. According to the New York City Fire Code, the recommended clearance from the top of stored warehouse goods to the sprinkler heads must be a minimum of ______ inches. 18.____

A. 2
B. 6
C. 12
D. 18

19. According to the City Fire Code, the recommended width of aisle space in a storage area must be a minimum of ______ foot(feet). 19.____

A. 1
B. 2
C. 3
D. 4

20. As a supervisor in charge of the total operation of a food supply warehouse, you find vandalism to be a potentially serious problem. On occasion, trespassers have gained entrance into the facility by climbing over an unprotected 8-foot fence surrounding the warehouse whose dimensions measure 100 feet by 100 feet. 20.____
Assuming that all of the following would be equally effective ways in preventing these breaches in security in the situation described above, which one would be LEAST costly?

A. Using two trained guard dogs to roam freely throughout the facility at night.
B. Hiring a security guard to patrol the facility after working hours.
C. Installing tape razor wire on top of the fence surrounding the facility.
D. Installing an electronic burglar alarm system requiring the installation of a new fence.

21. Assume that you are considering training one of your subordinates, Mr. Parks, to help you with your record keeping duties. You have decided on using the following four steps in your instruction: 21.____

I. Show Mr. Parks what has to be done.
II. Find out what Mr. Parks knows about the job.
III. Check to see how Mr. Parks is doing the job.
IV. Have Mr. Parks do the job himself.

Which one of the following shows the order of taking these steps that would be MOST effective in training Mr. Parks?

A. II, I, IV, III
B. III, II, I, IV
C. I, IV, III, II
D. IV, I, II, III

22. The one of the following which provides for efficient storage of loose hardware items such as nails, screws, nuts, bolts, and washers is a(n) 22.____

A. wire mesh basket
B. metal stack bin
C. open shelf unit
D. 55-gallon drum

23. A pallet load template is used to 23.____

A. construct new pallets
B. determine the floor load capacity in a warehouse
C. determine the size of the pallet needed for different-sized cartons
D. increase the allowable floor load in a warehouse

24. The fire extinguisher which is a pump-type tank water unit is used for fires involving all of the following EXCEPT 24.____

A. wood B. paper C. plastic D. grease

25. When storing 55-gallon drums outdoors, it is BEST to place the drums on their sides in order to 25.____

A. make them easier to store
B. prevent rain water from collecting on their tops
C. allow them to be stacked higher
D. keep the aisle space smaller

26. In the storage of a flammable liquid, the vapor density of the liquid is the MOST important factor in determining the 26.____

A. type of fire extinguisher to use
B. type of container used for storage
C. location of the ventilating outlets
D. usable life of a product

27. Of the following, the BEST place to store partially loaded pallets is 27.____

A. under fully loaded pallets
B. over other partially loaded pallets
C. on the top of stacked pallets
D. in the aisle space between two rows of stacked pallets

28. Of the following, the BEST reason why there should be a clearance on all sides of a stack of loaded pallets is to prevent the 28.____

A. tipping of the stack
B. crushing of the lower pallets
C. collection of moisture in between the stacks
D. dislocation of the surrounding stacks

29. Where forklift equipment is available, dunnage strips are MOST useful for which one of the following? 29.____

A. Storing a variety of stock items on loaded pallets
B. Stacking large containers, boxes, and crates
C. Storing pipes or other round items
D. Stacking items to be stored on shelves for a long time

30. Of the following, the MAIN advantage in the use of an *A* frame storage rack is that it provides 30.____

A. storage space for extremely large supplies of any item
B. storage space for any item that is to be shipped out immediately
C. a quick access to items that have to be inspected
D. maximum accessibility to smaller lots of bulk supplies

31. Which one of the following can be used to provide an efficient means of storing and stacking items that do not readily lend themselves to direct stacking? 31.____
A

A. pallet spear
B. collapsible pallet box
C. skid
D. two-way entry pallet

32. Of the following, the MAJOR benefit of good housekeeping in a warehouse is that it 32.____

A. allows workers more time to perform their regular duties
B. reduces the need for fire prevention and safety precautions
C. conserves space, equipment, time, and effort
D. reduces the need for identifying stock items and storage areas

33. Which one of the following is a good warehouse practice when receiving goods which will require inspection and tests? 33.____

A. Put the goods aside and have them properly labelled.
B. Leave the goods on the loading dock.
C. Place the goods into stock without delay.
D. Issue the goods to the user.

34. The one of the following which is a MAJOR advantage of a power-driven belt conveyor over a gravity-roller conveyor is that a power-driven belt conveyor can 34.____

A. be operated manually with equal effectiveness
B. move loads from a lower level to a higher level
C. be operated at any angle
D. be easily extended by adding sections

35. Of the following, the PRIMARY purpose for using pallets in handling stock is to provide 35.____

A. a large floor load capacity in a warehouse
B. easy storage of irregular items in a warehouse
C. efficient handling and storing of material in a warehouse
D. a safe working environment in a warehouse

36. Of the following, the FIRST consideration in determining whether a particular piece of materials handling equipment should be purchased for use in a large warehouse is the 36.____

A. qualifications of the personnel using the equipment
B. reliability of the manufacturer
C. availability of the replacement parts
D. allowable floor load capacity

37. When a shipment of goods is made to a warehouse, the person receiving the shipment should check the shipment against the freight bill or bill of lading. 37.____
The one of the following that thr receiver should note and sign for on the freight bill or bill of lading is the

A. size of the packages in the shipment
B. overage, shortage, or damage to the goods
C. outside identification on the packages
D. remaining number of shipments to be made

38. In planning how to handle the receipt of goods from a vendor efficiently, which one of the following would be the MOST useful information to have? The 38.____

A. unit price of the goods to be delivered
B. cost for shipping the goods
C. estimated time of arrival and the size of the delivery
D. type of material used in packing the goods

39. A using agency has just notified you that they will no longer be using a certain item due to changes in the agency's functions. There is a large supply of this item on hand in your warehouse, and two routine shipments are due next month from the vendor. Of the following, the MOST advisable action for you to take FIRST in this situation is to 39.____

A. determine if other city warehouses can use these supplies
B. store the supplies in an inactive section of the warehouse
C. prepare relinquishment forms to remove existing supplies for resale by the city
D. notify the proper authority to cancel any orders not yet received

40. A decision has been made to computerize your warehouse inventory control operation. Upon receiving your first computer readout, you notice that it indicates a shortage of a stock item that is usually in good supply. Of the following, the FIRST step you should take to deal with this matter is to 40.____

A. make a report of a possible theft
B. report to the computer center that they are in error
C. verify the information used for the computer readout
D. request that the computer be repaired

KEY (CORRECT ANSWERS)

1. B	11. B	21. A	31. A
2. C	12. B	22. B	32. C
3. C	13. D	23. C	33. A
4. B	14. D	24. D	34. B
5. C	15. B	25. B	35. C
6. B	16. A	26. C	36. D
7. D	17. C	27. C	37. B
8. A	18. D	28. D	38. C
9. B	19. C	29. B	39. D
10. A	20. C	30. D	40. C

EXAMINATION SECTION
TEST 1

DIRECTIONS: Each question or incomplete statement is followed by several suggested answers or completions. Select the one that BEST answers the question or completes the statement. *PRINT THE LETTER OF THE CORRECT ANSWER IN THE SPACE AT THE RIGHT.*

1. One of the results of understocking is that 1.____

   A. more money is tied up in stock
   B. stock must be ordered more frequently
   C. there is greater likelihood of obsolescence
   D. there is uneven distribution of materials in storage

2. Assume that your re-order point is obtained by multiplying the monthly rate of consumption by the lead time (in months) and adding the minimum balance. For a particular item, the re-order point is established at 200 units. 2.____
   If the lead time is 2 months and the minimum balance is 100, then the average monthly rate of consumption is

   A. 50 B. 100 C. 150 D. 200

3. If a certain item has shown no activity for two years, the MOST advisable action to take FIRST is to 3.____

   A. attempt to dispose of the item through salvage
   B. contact the using agencies or individuals to determine whether they can use the item
   C. contact the vendor to determine whether the item can be traded in
   D. write it off on the inventory control card

4. The MOST important information on an inventory control card is that which gives the ______ of the item. 4.____

   A. identity B. location
   C. rate of consumption D. vendor

5. A space 5 1/4 feet wide and 2 1/3 feet long has an area measuring MOST NEARLY ______ square feet. 5.____

   A. 9 B. 10 C. 11 D. 12

6. One man is able to load two 2 1/2-ton trucks in one hour. To load ten such trucks, it will take ten men ______ hour(s). 6.____

   A. 1/2 B. 1 C. 2 D. 2 1/2

7. If the average height of the stacks in your section of the storehouse is 10 feet, the area which will be occupied by 56,000 cubic feet of supplies is MOST likely to be 7.____

   A. 70' x 80' B. 60' x 90' C. 50' x 60' D. 560' x 100'

8. The number of cartons, each measuring two cubic feet, which can fit into a space which is 100 square feet in area and is 8 feet high is MOST NEARLY 8.____

A. 50 B. 200 C. 400 D. 800

9. When the floor area measures 200 feet by 200 feet and the maximum weight it can hold is 4,000 tons, then the safe floor load is _______ pounds per square foot. 9.____

A. 20 B. 160 C. 200 D. 400

10. A carton 1' x 1' x 3' measures _______ cubic yards. 10.____

A. 1/3 B. 1/9 C. 3 D. 9

11. You have received six cartons, each containing sixty boxes of staples, priced at $36.00 per carton. 11.____
The price per box is

A. $.10 B. $.60 C. $3.60 D. $6.00

12. The amount of space, in cubic feet, required to store 100 boxes each measuring 24" x 12" x 6" is MOST NEARLY 12.____

A. 10 B. 100 C. 168 D. 1008

13. Assume that it takes an average of two man-hours to stack 1 ton of certain supplies. In order to stack 30 tons, the number of men required to complete the job in ten hours is 13.____

A. 6 B. 10 C. 15 D. 30

14. An area measures 20 feet by 22 1/2 feet. The floor load is 100 pounds per square foot. The total weight that can be stored in this area is MOST NEARLY _______ pounds. 14.____

A. 450 B. 9,000 C. 22,500 D. 45,000

15. The price of a certain type of linoleum is $.20 per square foot. 15.____
The total cost of four pieces of 9' x 12' linoleum is MOST NEARLY

A. $21 B. $80 C. $86 D. $432

16. The number of board feet in a piece of lumber measuring 2 inches thick by 2 feet wide by 12 feet long is 16.____

A. 12 B. 16 C. 24 D. 48

17. If 39 3/8 ounces of a certain commodity are on hand and two requisitions are filled, one for 9 1/2 and one for 9 5/6 ounces, the number of ounces remaining are 17.____

A. 18 2/3 B. 19 1/3 C. 20 1/24 D. 20 3/4

18. In order to fill 96 bottles containing 3 fluid ounces each, the number of pints which would be needed is 18.____

A. 9 B. 18 C. 32 D. 36

19. If a section of a storeroom measures 29 feet 4 inches by 18 feet 3 inches, the total area is MOST NEARLY _______ square feet. 19.____

A. 523 B. 524 C. 535 D. 537

20. A discount of 1% is given on all purchases of over 100 brushes. An additional discount of 1% is given on all purchases of over 500 brushes. 20.____
If 600 brushes are purchased at a list price of $2.07 each, the total cost is MOST NEARLY

A. $1217 B. $1228 C. $1230 D. $2484

21. The following items are purchased: 30 locksets at $15.00 per dozen, and 10 gross of stove bolts at 1 1/2 cents each bolt. 21.____
The total cost is MOST NEARLY

A. $60 B. $180 C. $255 D. $470

22. The cost of one dozen pieces of screening, each measuring 4'6" by 5', at $.10 per square foot, is 22.____

A. $22.50 B. $25.00 C. $27.00 D. $27,60

23. The amount of turpentine on hand is 39 gallons. One requisition is filled for 3 1/2 gallons, three additional requisitions are filled for 3 quarts each, and six requisitions are filled for 1 pint each. 23.____
The quantity of turpentine remaining after all these requisitions have been filled is

A. 32 gal.
B. 32 gal. 1 qt.
C. 32 gal. 2 qts.
D. 32 gal. 3 qts.

24. A shelf is 30" wide and 20" deep. The shelf is filled solid with 500 boxes, each measuring 2" x 3" x 5". The distance from the shelf to the top of the stacked boxes is 24.____

A. 10" B. 25" C. 50" D. 60"

25. In order to check on a shipment of 1000 articles, a sampling of 100 articles was carefully inspected. 25.____
Of the sample, one article was wholly defective and 4 more were partly defective.
On this basis, the percentage of completely acceptable articles in the original shipment is probably MOST NEARLY

A. 5% B. 10% C. 95% D. 100%

26. The one of the following which is NOT the name of a type of screwdriver is 26.____

A. cabinet
B. flat-nose
C. knife handle
D. spiral ratchet

27. Pupil Dental Record forms are likely to be used in GREATEST quantities by the 27.____

A. Board of Education
B. Department of Health
C. Department of Hospitals
D. Department of Social Service

28. Crepe paper is likely to be requisitioned MOST frequently by the 28.____

A. Board of Education
B. Department of Public Events
C. Housing Authority
D. Transit Authority

29. Scalpels are likely to be requisitioned MOST frequently by the Department of 29.____

A. Correction
B. Health
C. Hospitals
D. Parks

30. Pruners are likely to be requisitioned MOST frequently by the 30.____

A. Department of Parks
B. Department of Sanitation
C. Reference Library
D. Transit Authority

31. Fustats are likely to be requisitioned MOST frequently by the 31.____

A. Department of Markets
B. Fire Department
C. Housing Authority
D. Police Department

32. Machine screws are usually purchased in large quantities by the 32.____

A. bushel B. gross C. pound D. score

33. A No. 10 can of fruit juice contains about 33.____

A. eight ounces
B. one pint
C. one quart
D. three quarts

34. Sulphuric acid is USUALLY purchased in large quantities by the 34.____

A. carboy B. drum C. gallon D. cylinder

35. The one of the following which is NOT a standard size of index card is 35.____

A. 3x5 B. 4x6 C. 5 x 7 D. 5 x 8

36. The label on a package of mimeograph paper reads: Size 8 1/2 x 11, Basis 20. *Basis 20* refers to the 36.____

A. color code for this type of paper
B. quality and finish of the paper
C. way in which the paper is packaged
D. weight of the paper

37. You tell a man to separate and store cans of paint in a certain way. The man then asks you, *Why do you want me to do it this way?* 37.____
You should answer his question by

A. advising him to figure out the reason himself
B. explaining to him why you want it done in that particular way
C. repeating your instructions more slowly
D. telling him to follow your instructions without asking any questions

38. Assume that an employee shows you that you have made an error in issuing certain instructions. You admit your error. 38.____
Such action on your part is desirable PRIMARILY because

A. the job may be done correctly
B. your men will be encouraged to make similar corrections in the future
C. you will gain a reputation for fairness
D. your men will realize that you will not make errors of this type in the future

39. Assume that you have just been promoted. Your supervisor gives you detailed oral instructions as to how a particular category of stock should be stored. At the conclusion of his instructions, you realize that you do not fully understand how your supervisor wishes to have the stock stored. 39.____
Under these circumstances, you should

   A. ask an experienced worker to clarify your supervisor's instructions
   B. ask your supervisor to clarify anything that you do not understand
   C. ask your supervisor to put his instructions in writing
   D. carry out your supervisor's instructions as best as you can

40. You have reason to believe that one of your men is taking merchandise which does not belong to him from the storehouse. You question the man about this. He tells you that he borrowed the merchandise and intends to return it. Under these Circumstances, you should probably 40.____

   A. disregard the matter until such time as you have evidence which will stand up in court
   B. offer to accompany the man to his home to pick up the property in question
   C. report the matter to your supervisor
   D. tell the man to return the property as soon as he has finished using it

41. A truck which must be unloaded immediately arrives at the storehouse. You issue instructions to your crew as to how this should be done. One of your men strongly objects and says that your instructions are wrong. You listen to his reasons but you still think that you are right. Under these circumstances, you should 41.____

   A. ask for opinions from the other men in the crew as to how the job should be done
   B. contact another worker to get his opinion
   C. refer the matter to your supervisor for his decision
   D. tell the men to unload the truck in accordance with your instructions

42. Whenever you give an assignment to one of your experienced men, he asks you a great many questions about it although he has successfully performed similar assignments in the past. The time you spend in answering his many questions about minor details takes you away from more important work. 42.____
Under these circumstances, you should probably FIRST

   A. answer his questions in such a way that he will be discouraged from asking further questions
   B. ask the man to ask his questions of one of his fellow employees
   C. assure the man of your confidence in his ability to carry out the assignment
   D. tell the man that if the assignment is too difficult you will give it to someone who does not raise so many questions

43. You have reason to believe that one of the men in your crew gossips about you behind your back. 43.____
Under these circumstances, it is usually BEST to

   A. attempt to find out which of your men believes the gossip
   B. find out what the man's weak points are and bring them to the attention of your crew

C. ignore the matter
D. speak to the man about it and tell him to stop

44. Your supervisor gives you an assignment which you believe you cannot do since you do not have a sufficient number of men. You explain this to your supervisor but he tells you to get the job done. 44.____
You should

A. do the best you can and keep your supervisor informed of the progress you are making
B. report the matter to your main office
C. insist that your supervisor give you his instructions in writing
D. wait until your supervisor gives you more men before taking any action to carry out the assignment

45. Your crew consistently performs more work than the crew headed by another worker. The other worker tells you that the high performance of your crew makes his crew *look bad.* 45.____
Under these circumstances, it would be BEST for you to

A. ignore the matter and have your crew continue working as before
B. report the matter to your supervisor for disciplinary action
C. slow your crew down somewhat to show the other man that you are willing to cooperate with him
D. slow your crew down to the level of the other crew

46. Two of your men frequently argue with each other so that the work of your crew is disrupted. 46.____
You should FIRST

A. attempt to find out why the men argue with each other
B. speak to the two men privately regarding their possible transfer to another crew
C. submit a report to your supervisor setting forth the facts
D. tell both men that unless they stop arguing you will see that they are given below-standard service ratings

47. One of your men asks you to put him in for an above-standard service rating. His work has been good but it has not been above-standard. 47.____
You should tell the man that

A. he has done good work but that in your judgment his work has not been above-standard
B. if you recommend him for an above-standard service rating, you will have to do the same thing for most of the others in your crew
C. you cannot discuss the matter with him but that you will discuss it with your supervisor
D. you will speak to the other men in the crew and if no one objects you will recommend him for a higher service rating

48. You receive a memorandum from your supervisor in which he instructs you to make a large number of changes in the procedures for storing materials. 48.____
The BEST way to bring these changes to the attention of your crew is to

A. post the memorandum on the bulletin board where everyone can read it
B. meet individually with each member of your staff to discuss the changes
C. hold a meeting with your crew and explain the changes to them
D. see to it that the memorandum is circulated to and initialled by each member of the crew

49. Although you have frequently spoken to one of your men regarding the proper way of lifting heavy objects, he persists in ignoring your instructions. He says that he knows the proper way of lifting, that you do not, and that he does not intend to hurt himself by following your instructions. 49.____
Of the following, the BEST course of action for you to take is to

A. assign the man to tasks which do not involve heavy lifting
B. ignore the matter as long as the man does not hurt himself
C. put your instructions on how to lift in writing and give a copy of your instructions to each man in the crew
D. report the matter to your supervisor

50. You assign a man to take inventory of a certain item. The man gives you a figure which seems too high. Of the following, the BEST course of action for you to take is to 50.____

A. accept the figure given to you by the man if he is willing to initial it
B. accompany the man while he takes inventory again
C. ask the man to take inventory again and tell him why
D. take inventory yourself

KEY (CORRECT ANSWERS)

1.	B	11.	B	21.	A	31.	C	41.	D
2.	A	12.	B	22.	C	32.	B	42.	C
3.	B	13.	A	23.	C	33.	D	43.	C
4.	A	14.	D	24.	B	34.	A	44.	A
5.	D	15.	C	25.	C	35.	C	45.	A
6.	A	16.	D	26.	B	36.	D	46.	A
7.	A	17.	C	27.	A	37.	B	47.	A
8.	C	18.	B	28.	A	38.	A	48.	C
9.	C	19.	C	29.	C	39.	B	49.	D
10.	B	20.	A	30.	A	40.	C	50.	C

EXAMINATION SECTION
TEST 1

DIRECTIONS: Each question or incomplete statement is followed by several suggested answers or completions. Select the one that BEST answers the question or completes the statement. *PRINT THE LETTER OF THE CORRECT ANSWER IN THE SPACE AT THE RIGHT.*

1. For the GREATEST economy in transporting stock, one should 1._____

   A. divide the load into as many easily managed units as possible
   B. replace machines with men whenever possible
   C. transport as large a load as possible at one time
   D. utilize conveyor belts for most transporting

2. Assume that a new piece of equipment has been devised that would cut the labor cost of a certain major operation 75% and the time 50%. The monetary savings to the city would be such that the machine would pay for itself in one year. However, the old equipment is still in good working condition. 2._____
   The MOST advisable recommendation to make is that the

   A. *new* equipment be purchased
   B. *new* equipment be purchased only if the old equipment can be sold at a reasonable price
   C. *new* equipment be rented
   D. *old* equipment be retained until there is moderate deterioration

3. Economy in handling stock can be measured BEST in terms of the 3._____

   A. cost of the equipment used
   B. cost of stock-handling operations
   C. overhead cost plus depreciation of equipment
   D. salaries being paid to the men

4. It is MOST economical and efficient to have good lighting available in 4._____

   A. all parts of the storehouse
   B. packing areas only
   C. receiving areas only
   D. storage areas only

5. If a great deal of heavy work must be completed by men under your supervision, it is MOST advisable, when possible, to 5._____

   A. give frequent rest periods
   B. have the men work overtime
   C. have the men listen to lively music while working
   D. shorten the lunch hour

6. A storehouse USUALLY operates at GREATEST efficiency when it stores _______ stock than it is designed to hold. 6._____

   A. slightly less
   B. slightly more
   C. substantially more
   D. the exact amount of

7. Usually, a report should be prepared with AT LEAST 7.____

A. one copy so that there is a copy for future reference
B. two copies so that the report can be sent to more than one person
C. two copies so that there is an extra copy for your supervisor
D. three copies so that there will be sufficient copies if they are needed

8. Of the following, the one which can MOST easily be increased or improved in an employee by his foreman or supervisor is 8.____

A. ability to learn
B. aptitude
C. common sense
D. knowledge

9. Two men under your supervision who are required to work together are not able to get along with each other. You have attempted to remedy this situation but without any success. One is an older man who has been in the section for many years, and the other is a recently-appointed younger man. Both men are capable employees. 9.____
Of the following, the MOST advisable course of action for you to take is to recommend that the

A. older man be transferred
B. two men be given below-average service ratings
C. younger man be discharged at the end of his probationary period
D. younger man be transferred

10. Inefficient scheduling of work should be suspected when one notes that there are several men 10.____

A. absent from work
B. in the rest room
C. loading a truck
D. waiting to use equipment

11. *It is better to haul than to carry.* 11.____
The PRIMARY reason for this statement is that

A. stock should not be placed on top of any movable equipment
B. stockmen should not be allowed to carry stock for any great distance
C. the same power can usually pull more than it can carry
D. there is less danger of damage when stock is hauled

12. After you have given a newly-appointed subordinate complete instructions on how to use a handtruck, you should usually 12.____

A. assign him to work with another subordinate
B. go over the instructions once more
C. let him use the handtruck while you watch him
D. tell him about the importance of the work

13. One of your subordinates tells you that he wants to submit a suggestion to the suggestion program regarding the operation of the storeroom but that he wants your advice first. The MOST advisable course of action for you to take is to 13.____

A. advise him that any suggestions concerning the storeroom should be made directly to you
B. give him advice provided he includes your name on the suggestion

C. give him the advice he needs
D. tell him that it would not be fair if you were to give him any help

14. Assume that you are in charge of one section of a storehouse. When the man in charge of an adjoining section resigns, you are asked to assume that job in addition to your own. After several weeks, you find that it is impossible for you to provide adequate supervision for both sections.
Of the following, the BEST course of action for you to take is to 14.____

A. ask your supervisor for a transfer
B. assign one subordinate in each section the job of supervision
C. divide your time between the two sections
D. inform your supervisor of the facts

15. Your subordinates tell you that, in your absence, your supervisor gave them orders which differed from those which you had given them.
In this case, you should 15.____

A. discuss the matter with your subordinates to determine which orders are correct
B. discuss the matter with your supervisor
C. tell your subordinates to follow your orders
D. tell your subordinates to follow your supervisor's orders

16. Assume that one of your subordinates made an error in recording an issue of stock. The mistake was found and corrected, but your subordinate seems rather depressed about the matter.
Of the following, the MOST advisable course of action for you to take is to 16.____

A. ignore the entire situation unless it happens again
B. praise him
C. reprimand him mildly
D. show him how he can avoid such a mistake in the future

17. Assume that you have the following equipment available: two forklift trucks, one tractor, six trailers, and four handtrucks.
In order to move twenty pallet loads 200 yards in a storehouse, it would be MOST advisable for you to use the 17.____

A. forklift trucks
B. forklift trucks, the tractor, and the trailers
C. handtrucks, the tractor, and the trailers
D. tractor and the trailers

18. Small cartons to be stored for a period of a year would usually be BEST stored on 18.____

A. dollies B. pallets C. the floor D. trailers

19. The one of the following types of equipment which should generally be used to collect a small number of items from various parts of the storehouse for a single shipment is a 19.____

A. four-wheel truck
B. pallet
C. skid
D. two-wheel truck

20. In a large city storehouse, main aisles used for movement of materials should usually be NOT less than _______ ft. 20.____

A. 1 B. 2 C. 4 D. 6

21. An aisle used only as a fire aisle should be APPROXIMATELY _______ feet wide. 21.____

A. 2 B. 5 C. 8 D. 10

22. When a perishable commodity is received at the storeroom, the factor which is generally LEAST important to consider when deciding where to store it is the 22.____

A. activity of the commodity
B. size and weight of the commodity
C. temperature and humidity of the storage areas
D. total storage capacity of the storeroom

23. Ten cartons of a certain item are stacked on each of ten pallets standing in a row. Assume that the men and equipment mentioned below are available. 23.____
In order to move the cartons, with or without the pallets, from their place in the storehouse into a waiting truck, a distance of 25 yards, it would be MOST efficient to

A. form a line of men to pass the cartons into the truck
B. have a forklift truck take each pallet load separately and load it on the truck
C. have one man move each pallet load with a hand lift pallet truck
D. transfer the cartons from the pallets to a single tractor trailer train and then load them on the truck

24. The one of the following circumstances in which it would be MOST appropriate to use a fixed-platform power truck rather than a forklift truck is when 24.____

A. loading a railroad car
B. miscellaneous small items must be selected for a single shipment
C. the load must be carried over a long distance
D. there is a shortage of manpower

25. Storing small items in their original containers is a 25.____

A. *bad* practice because it encourages laziness
B. *bad* practice because it is disorderly
C. *good* practice because it decreases handling
D. *good* practice because it eliminates the need for shelves and bins

KEY (CORRECT ANSWERS)

1. C
2. A
3. B
4. A
5. A
6. D
7. A
8. D
9. D
10. D
11. C
12. C
13. C
14. D
15. B
16. D
17. B
18. B
19. A
20. D
21. A
22. D
23. B
24. B
25. C

TEST 2

DIRECTIONS: Each question or incomplete statement is followed by several suggested answers or completions. Select the one that BEST answers the question or completes the statement. *PRINT THE LETTER OF THE CORRECT ANSWER IN THE SPACE AT THE RIGHT.*

1. Assume that you have to move two cartons to a location about 50 feet away. Each carton weighs 10 pounds and measures 2' x 4' x 4'. 1.____
Of the following, the method of moving the cartons which would ordinarily be BEST is to

   A. have two men carry each carton
   B. make one trip using a two-wheel handtruck
   C. make two trips using a two-wheel handtruck
   D. put both cartons on a four-wheel handtruck

2. Assume that you have to move two cartons to a location about 25 feet away. Each carton weighs 10 pounds and measures 6" x 12" x 18". 2.____
Of the following, the method of moving the cartons which would ordinarily be BEST is to

   A. have one man carry both cartons in one trip
   B. have one man make two trips
   C. put both cartons on a four-wheel handtruck
   D. put both cartons on a two-wheel handtruck

3. Assume that you have to move twenty 10-pound cartons to a location about 100 feet away. 3.____
Of the following, the method of moving the cartons which would ordinarily be BEST is to

   A. get a team of men to carry them by hand
   B. load them on a pallet and use a forklift truck
   C. load them on a skid and push the skid
   D. make a line of men and pass them from hand to hand

4. Assume that you have to move fifty pallets from one location in the warehouse to another about 250 feet away. Of the following, the equipment that you would need to do the job MOST efficiently is 4.____

   A. forklift truck, tractor, trailers
   B. four-wheel handtruck, portable elevator
   C. two-wheel handtruck, tractor, trailers
   D. two-wheel handtruck, trailers

5. The principle of *first-in, first-out* should generally be applied 5.____

   A. only to commodities subject to deterioration
   B. only to dated commodities
   C. only to perishable commodities
   D. to most commodities

6. A worker who is lifting a heavy object from the floor to a shoulder height position should preferably 6.____

   A. bend his knees, keep his back straight, and jerk the object to shoulder height in one quick motion
   B. bend his knees, keep his back straight, and lift to shoulder height in a slow continuous motion
   C. lift the object waist high, rest one end of it on a ledge, and then, while bending the knees, raise it to shoulder height
   D. lift the object waist high, rest one end of it on a ledge, and then, while keeping the knees straight, raise it to shoulder height

7. You have in stock a full drum of liquid which is lying on its side. You assign two men to stand it upright. 7.____
   The proper position for the men to take is for ______ to stand ______ of the drum.

   A. both; at the bottom end
   B. both; at the top end
   C. each; on opposite ends
   D. each; on opposite sides

8. Assume that you are employed in a well organized storehouse. Your stock records indicate that 450 units of a certain commodity are in stock. You count these items on a shelf and find only 175. 8.____
   The MOST advisable action for you to take FIRST is to

   A. consult the locator system
   B. count these items again
   C. recompute the stock balance
   D. report the shortage

9. A certain item is stored in a number of locations throughout a storeroom. You have counted the items in each location and added the numbers to get the total. 9.____
   Of the following, the BEST way to make sure that your figures are correct is to

   A. add the numbers again, using a different method
   B. add the numbers again, using the same method
   C. count the items again and recompute
   D. move all the items to one location

10. In taking inventory, you count much more of a certain iten than is shown on the inventory card. 10.____
    Of the following, the MOST advisable action for you to take FIRST is to

    A. put an adjusting entry on the inventory card
    B. refer the matter to your supervisor
    C. review all requisitions since the last inventory record
    D. recheck the figures on the card

11. Assume that paper is issued at the rate of 500 reams per month. Three-hole punches are issued at the rate of 1 a month. 11.___
Of the following alternatives, it would probably be MOST practical and economic to order

A. 500 reams per month and one three-hole punch per month
B. 1,500 reams four times a year and 12 three-hole punches once a year
C. 2,000 reams three times a year and 60 three-hole punches once every 5 years
D. 18,000 reams once every 3 years and 36 three-hole punches once every 3 years

12. Assume that the price of an item is much lower during the months of June, July, and August However, you issue it throughout the year at the rate of 100 per month. The delivery time is one month, and you keep a one-month's reserve on hand at all times. You have enough room for 600 items. 12.___
Of the following, it would ordinarily be BEST for you to order

A. 200 in June, 500 in August, and 500 in January
B. 400 in June, 400 in August, and 400 in December
C. 600 in July and 600 in December
D. 500 in June, 200 in July, and 500 in August

13. Assume that one of the items which you stock is issued only during April, May, and June at the rate of 400 per month. You keep a one-month's supply on hand at all times, although you have sufficient room for an unlimited supply. The delivery time is one month. 13.___
Assuming that there are sufficient funds available at all times, it would probably be BEST for you to order

A. 100 each month of the year
B. 400 in March, 400 in April, and 400 in May
C. 400 in April, 400 in May, and 400 in June
D. 1,200 in March

14. Assume that you stock an item which deteriorates rapidly after 2 months. This item is issued at an average rate of 100 per month. The delivery time is one month. You keep a reserve supply of 20. 14.___
If these figures are maintained, you should order ______ iteris once ______ month(s).

A. 100; a
B. 200; every two
C. 220; every two
D. 300; every three

15. Assume that you have 50 boxes of a particular item on hand. The minimum order point is 100, and you have already ordered 300 boxes, which is the usual 3-months' supply. This order has not yet been delivered, and you have just received a special requisition for an additional 300 boxes. 15.___
Of the following, the MOST advisable action for you to take is to order

A. 300 boxes immediately
B. 300 boxes as soon as your outstanding order has been received
C. 600 boxes immediately
D. 600 boxes at the end of the present 3-month period

16. When a new model of a certain item is manufactured, you still have in stock a number of items of the old model. The old model is usable, but all the requisitions call for the new model.
Asking the requesting agencies or individuals to accept the old model instead is 16.____

A. *desirable* because the best items should be issued last
B. *desirable* because you will not be left with obsolete stock
C. *undesirable* because it is interfering with their prerogatives
D. *undesirable* because they should not be penalized for your errors

17. You are planning to submit an initial order for a new item. You estimate that you will issue 10 per month, and you want to have a one month's supply in reserve. You will reorder this item every three months.
Your initial order should be for 17.____

A. 10 B. 20 C. 30 D. 40

18. You have room in the storehouse for 1,000 cartons of a certain item. Assume that you issue 100 boxes per month and always keep a one-month's supply in reserve. You order supplies every six months. Delivery time is thirty days.
Of the following, the MOST appropriate amount to order under usual circumstances is 18.____

A. 500 B. 600 C. 700 D. 1,000

19. The PRINCIPAL disadvantage of having an order-picker fill two or more orders at one time is that 19.____

A. more equipment is needed
B. the order-picker will resent the burden
C. the work must be scheduled more precisely
D. there is greater chance of error

20. Of the following, the MOST important reason for having a physical inventory as well as a perpetual inventory is that a physical inventory 20.____

A. enables a physical inspection of the items to determine their condition
B. familiarizes the men with the stock
C. gives a count of the number of items actually on hand
D. provides an opportunity to clean up the area

21. Of the following conditions, the one which is properly represented by an annual stock turnover of 2.0 is ______ original stock has been replaced ______. 21.____

A. half of the; during the year
B. the; once during the year
C. the; twice during the year
D. the; once every two months

22. Of the following kinds of items, the one for which frequent inspections are MOST necessary is the item which is 22.____

A. dated B. heavy C. plastic D. small

23. Of the following items, the one for which physical counts should be made MOST frequently is 23.__

A. nails B. pipes C. valves D. wrenches

24. In order to avoid any interruption in normal storehouse operations during physical inventory, it would be necessary to 24.__

A. close each section as it is inventoried
B. close the storehouse during inventory
C. inventory only on alternate days
D. inventory after working hours or on weekends

25. It would be desirable to reduce stock levels to a one month period when the item is 25.__

A. *expensive* and can be readily obtained
B. *expensive* and difficult to obtain
C. *inexpensive* and can be readily obtained
D. *inexpensive* and difficult to obtain

KEY (CORRECT ANSWERS)

1.	D	11.	B
2.	A	12.	B
3.	B	13.	D
4.	A	14.	A
5.	D	15.	A
6.	C	16.	B
7.	D	17.	D
8.	A	18.	B
9.	C	19.	D
10.	D	20.	C

21. C
22. A
23. D
24. D
25. A

EXAMINATION SECTION
TEST 1

DIRECTIONS: Each question or incomplete statement is followed by several suggested answers or completions. Select the one that BEST answers the question or completes the statement. *PRINT THE LETTER OF THE CORRECT ANSWER IN THE SPACE AT THE RIGHT.*

1. Of the following, the hazard MOST likely to damage rubber tubes in storage is 1.____

   A. breakage
   B. combustion
   C. corrosion
   D. deterioration

2. Of the following, the hazard MOST likely to damage vacuum tubes in storage is 2.____

   A. breakage
   B. corrosion
   C. deterioration
   D. evaporation

3. In checking large numbers of incoming supplies of a single item, the BEST practice to follow is to 3.____

   A. count the total number of containers received and only count the number of units in some of the containers
   B. count the total number of containers received only in those shipments where there is some doubt
   C. open all exterior containers received and count the number of containers inside when there are interior containers
   D. open all exterior and interior containers received and count the exact number of units

4. Some experts advise that barrels containing liquids should be turned occasionally. The BEST reason for this is to 4.____

   A. enable a check of the condition of the barrel
   B. enable a check of the condition of the contents
   C. keep the contents well mixed
   D. prevent the wood from drying out

5. For day-to-day protection when working in a room or enclosure containing combustible or explosive gases or gasolines, it would be MOST advisable to wear 5.____

   A. a general purpose gas mask
   B. a synthetic rubber suit
   C. non-sparking shoes
   D. rubber-framed goggles

6. The one of the following which is NOT recommended as a method of reducing the possibility of spontaneous combustion of burlap bags is to 6.____

   A. air them out before stacking
   B. dampen them slightly before stacking
   C. keep them off concrete floors
   D. keep them away from brick walls

7. When oxygen is leaking from a gas cylinder and the valve cannot close properly, the MOST advisable course of action to take while waiting for the valve to be repaired is to 7._____

   A. evacuate the building
   B. have it sent to a using agency before more oxygen is lost
   C. place the cylinder in the room with the poorest ventilation
   D. remove the cylinder from the building

8. Assume that you have to move four cartons to a location about 35 feet away. Each carton weighs 20 pounds and measures 2' x 8' x 4'. 8._____
   Of the following, the method of moving the cartons which would ordinarily be BEST is to

   A. have a team of two men make four trips
   B. have two teams of two men each carry two cartons
   C. make one trip using a four-wheel handtruck
   D. make one trip using a two-wheel handtruck

9. Assume that you have to move one carton to a location about 15 feet away. The carton weighs about 30 pounds and measures 8" x 18" x 24". 9._____
   Of the following, the method of moving the carton which would ordinarily be BEST is to

   A. have one man carry it
   B. have two men carry it
   C. put it on a two-wheel handtruck
   D. put it on a four-wheel handtruck

10. Assume that you have to move ten 45 pound cartons to a location about 75 feet away. Each carton measures 24" x 24" x 24". 10._____
    Of the following, the method of moving the cartons which would ordinarily be BEST is to

    A. load them on a pallet and use a forklift truck
    B. load them on a skid and push the skid
    C. load them on a trailer and pull it with a tractor
    D. use a portable conveyor

Questions 11-16.

DIRECTIONS: Questions 11 through 16 are to be answered SOLELY on the basis of the following table.

REPORT OF SEMI-ANNUAL INVENTORY

Article	Physical Inventory				Perpetual Inventory		Adjustment	
	Unit	Qty.	Price	Amt.	Qty.	Amt.	Qty.	Amt.
Batteries, flashlight	ea.	63	.08	5.04	60	14.80	+3	+.24
Bolts, flat head with square nuts, 100 in box	box	23	1.47	33.80	25	36.75		
Fuse, 15 amp, 4 in box	box	80	.07	5.60	80	5.60		
Fuse, 20 amp, 4 in box	box	77	.07	5.39	80	5.60	3	.21
Tape, friction, 50 ft. to a roll	roll	45	.22	9.90	45	9.90		
Washers, 100 in can								
1/8" beveled	can	35	.32	11.20	35	11.20		
3/8" beveled	can	41	.33	13.53	45	14.85	4	1.32
Totals				84.47		88.70		

11. In the above report, for which item is there an INCORRECT entry? 11.____

    A. 15 amp. fuses
    B. Friction tape
    C. Flashlight batteries
    D. 1/8" washers

12. In the above report, adjustments were omitted for ______ article(s). 12.____

    A. one B. two C. three D. four

13. After all appropriate entries have been made in the Adjustment column, the total which must be deducted from the book value of the inventory is 13.____

    A. $1.53 B. $1.77 C. $4.23 D. $4.71

14. The quantities shown in Perpetual Inventory exceed those shown in Physical Inventory by a total of 14.____

    A. 4 B. 6 C. 10 D. 12

15. The cost of ten washers, 1/8" beveled, is MOST NEARLY 15.____

    A. $.003 B. $.032 C. $.320 D. $3.20

16. The cost of 24 fuses is MOST NEARLY 16.____

    A. $.28 B. $.42 C. $.80 D. $1.68

17. Assume that you are in charge of a group of four men who are to carry an oak beam measuring 8" x 8" x 18' from one point to another. 17.____
Of the following, the BEST method of carrying the beam is to have

A. the men arrange themselves at equal distances along one side of the beam and carry the beam at their sides
B. the men arrange themselves at equal distances on opposite sides of the beam and carry the beam at waist height
C. the men arrange themselves in order of height along the beam so that the beam may be carried on the shoulders of all of the men
D. two men stand at one end of the beam and two men at the other end in order to lift the beam on to the shoulders of the two strongest men

18. Although the old model of a certain item has been replaced by a new model which is interchangeable with the old model, most requisitions call specifically for the old model. Since your stock of the old model is almost depleted, it would be MOST advisable for you to 18.____

A. establish a carefully regulated system of priorities based on need
B. inform the source of your supply of the continued demand for the old model
C. inform the using agencies or individuals of the feasibility of substituting the new model
D. substitute the new model whenever the old model is called for

19. An assistant stockman is assigned by you to take physical inventory of a particular small part stored in several open boxes. This part is of uniform size and is packaged 100 to a box. He returns in an unusually short time with the count. His explanation for his speed is that he consolidated all the items as much as possible so that all except one box were full. He multiplied 100 by the number of boxes and added the number of additional parts left. 19.____
Of the following, the MOST advisable course of action for you to take is to

A. compliment him on his efficiency
B. explain the proper way of taking inventory
C. have him watch a more experienced worker take inventory
D. suggest that he ask permission before changing procedure

20. In determining the number of months of supply to be ordered at one time, the LEAST important of the following factors is the 20.____

A. average market price
B. deterioration rate
C. discount for quantity
D. money available for purchasing

21. A check during physical inventory has revealed that many of the bottles of alcohol do not contain sixteen ounces as indicated on the labels. 21.____
Of the following, the MOST advisable action to take FIRST is to

A. check future shipments by the vendor immediately upon their arrival
B. see if the bottles are tightly capped
C. see if the cartons are wet
D. question your subordinates about the situation

22. Of the following, the FIRST thing which should be done in order to determine the reason for a discrepancy between the perpetual inventory card and the bin card or other similar record is to 22.____

A. check the original requisitions
B. compare each transaction listed on both cards
C. ascertain whether any stock has been transferred to another warehouse
D. question all personnel involved

23. Items such as tools are sometimes issued on a temporary basis and are to be returned after use so that they may be issued again when needed. In such cases, a record of each withdrawal 23.____

A. need not be kept
B. should be made on an inventory card
C. should be made on a locator card
D. should be made on a separate register

24. Assume that you have 100 boxes of a particular item on hand. Since this is the minimum order point, you have already ordered 300 boxes, which is the usual 6 months' supply. This order has not yet been delivered, and you have just received a requisition for 1,000 boxes.
Of the following, the MOST advisable action for you to take FIRST is to 24.____

A. order an additional 1,000 boxes
B. order an additional 1,300 boxes
C. ascertain the reason for such a requisition
D. inform the ordering agency that the requisition cannot be filled immediately

Questions 25-27.

DIRECTIONS: Questions 25 through 27 are based on the following method of obtaining a reorder point: multiply the monthly rate of consumption by the lead time (in months) and add the minimum balance.

25. If the reorder point is 250 units, the lead time is 2 months, and the average monthly rate of consumption is 75 units, then the minimum balance is ______ units. 25.____

A. 75 B. 100 C. 150 D. 250

26. If the lead time is 30 days, the minimum balance is 200 units, and the average monthly rate of consumption is 100 units, then the reorder point is ______ units. 26.____

A. 100 B. 200 C. 300 D. 400

27. If the reorder point is 300 units, the lead time is 2 months, and the minimum balance is 100 units, then the average monthly rate of consumption is ______ units. 27.____

A. 50 B. 100 C. 200 D. 300

28. You are planning to submit an initial order for a new item . You estimate that you will issue 100 per month, and you want to have a two-month supply in reserve. You will reorder this item every six months. Your initial order should be for 28.____

A. 200 B. 600 C. 700 D. 800

29. For a particular item, the reorder point is established at 585. If the average rate of consumption is 130 and the lead time is 3 months, then the amount which should be on hand when the new delivery is received is 29.____

A. 130 B. 195 C. 260 D. 325

30. You have room in the storehouse for 750 cartons of a certain item. Assume that you issue 125 cartons per month and keep a one-month supply in reserve. Delivery time is thirty days. 30.____
Which of the following would it be MOST appropriate to order under these conditions?
_______ every _______ months.

A. 250; 3 B. 500; 3 C. 375; 4 D. 500; 4

31. Using maximum loads when transporting stock is 31.____

A. *desirable* because it results in fewer trips
B. *desirable* because it simplifies accounting and clerical work
C. *undesirable* because it shortens the life of the equipment
D. *undesirable* because it strains the capacity of the workers

32. Of the following, the BEST single basis for determining the desirability of purchasing new stock-handling equipment is the 32.____

A. ability of the workers to handle the equipment
B. condition of the present equipment
C. estimated savings in costs
D. size of the warehouse or stock facility

33. Frequent rest periods are MOST desirable when 33.____

A. the men have been doing a good job
B. the morale of the men is low
C. there is a great deal of heavy work
D. there is not too much work

34. In terms of plant economy, a storehouse is operating at GREATEST efficiency when it stores _______ stock that it is designed to hold. 34.____

A. 10% less B. 10% more
C. 50% more D. the exact amount of

35. Of the following, the one which a foreman or supervisor can MOST readily increase or improve is an employee's ability to 35.____

A. get along with his fellow workers
B. perform technical aspects of his job
C. supervise others
D. use good judgment in unusual situations

36. On one day, a certain piece of stock-handling equipment is not used at all. On the next day, several men are waiting to use it. 36.____
This situation can BEST be corrected by

A. having the men do the work manually
B. keeping additional equipment available

C. posting a schedule for the use of the equipment
D. rearranging the work of the men

37. Despite all your efforts to streamline the work and make it more efficient, there still seems to be more work than you and your men can handle in a normal work week. The MOST advisable course of action for you to take FIRST is to 37.____

A. discuss the matter with your supervisor
B. request more mechanical equipment
C. request permission for overtime work
D. tell your men that everyone will have to work a little harder

38. Assume that a subordinate tells you that he has made a mistake in filling out certain records. The MOST advisable action for you to take FIRST is to 38.____

A. explain how the job should have been done
B. get another subordinate to do the job correctly
C. tell him how to correct his mistake
D. tell him to forget it but to do it correctly next time

39. Your supervisor gives you instructions which you feel are contrary to good storage procedure. The MOST advisable action for you to take FIRST is to 39.____

A. attempt to get additional support for your point of view
B. follow his instructions without question
C. suggest your method of doing the work
D. say nothing but do the job the way you feel it should be done

40. You have reason to believe that one of your men is taking home merchandise from the storehouse. You question the man about this. He shows you that it was obsolete material of no value which was not salvageable and was about to be discarded. Under these circumstances, the MOST appropriate action for you to take is to 40.____

A. have him return the merchandise
B. report the matter to your supervisor
C. say nothing further
D. tell the man that he should have asked your permission

41. Three new men have just been assigned to work under your supervision. Every time you give them an assignment, one of these men asks you several questions. Of the following, the MOST advisable action for you to take is to 41.____

A. assure him of your confidence in his ability to carry out the assignment correctly without asking so many questions
B. have all three men listen to your answers to these questions
C. point out that the other two men do the job without asking so many questions
D. tell him to see if he can get the answers from other workers before coming to you

42. One of the men in your crew has continually been making derogatory statements about the personal life of one of the other men. 42.____
Of the following, it would probably be MOST advisable for you to

A. attempt to obtain a transfer for the man who is the subject of the derogatory statements
B. ignore the matter unless it has any effect on the work
C. point out to your crew some of the weak spots in the character of the man who is making derogatory statements
D. tell the man to stop making derogatory statements

43. Two of your subordinates suggest that you recommend a third man for an above-standard service rating because of his superior work. 43.____
You should

A. ask the two subordinates whether the third man knows that they intended to discuss this matter with you
B. explain to the two subordinates that an above-standard service rating for one man would have a detrimental effect on many of the other men
C. recommend the man for an above-standard service rating if there is sufficient justification for it
D. tell the two subordinates that the matter of service ratings is not their concern

44. At a meeting with your subordinates, which you have called in order to determine the best ways of dealing with some departmental policies, some of the men interrupt with comments and suggestions. 44.____
Of the following, the MOST advisable course of action for you to take in MOST cases is to

A. encourage full but orderly participation by all the men
B. end the meeting and issue a bulletin instead
C. tell them to hold their comments and questions until after you have finished
D. tell those who interrupt that they are being unfair to the others

45. When one of your subordinates takes unusually long lunch hours, you tell him that this practice must stop. 45.____
Of the following, the BEST reason for speaking to him about this is that

A. he will take even longer lunch hours unless you speak to him
B. morale of your other subordinates may be impaired unless the situation is corrected
C. work cannot be done in time unless the practice is discontinued
D. your other subordinates will take the same amount of time for lunch as he does

46. You have just been assigned a new employee who has had a college education but has had no experience in stock work. Of the following, the BEST course of action for you to take is to 46.____

A. attempt to have him transferred as soon as possible
B. explain to him that he probably would not like the work
C. make special efforts to ease his relationships with the other workers
D. treat him the same as you would treat any other new worker

47. The morale of your subordinates seems unusually high. They tell you that it is because they have heard that one of them is to get a provisional promotion. You know definitely that this is not true. 47.____
The MOST advisable action for you to take is to

A. act as if you are happy to hear the good news
B. let the situation take its normal course
C. report the matter to your supervisor
D. tell them that, so far as you know, the rumor is not justified

48. In most cases, the FIRST step to take in the event of serious injury in the storeroom is to 48.____

A. search the employee for instructions pertaining to medical care
B. send for medical help
C. take the employee to a hospital
D. treat the injury

49. An employee has accidentally cut his arm and is bleeding profusely. 49.____
The one of the following which should NOT be done is to

A. apply pressure above the injury
B. give the employee a mild stimulant
C. keep the employee at complete rest
D. raise the bleeding part

50. When gasoline and all other highly inflammable substances are stored outdoors, the *No Smoking* rule should be 50.____

A. observed for indoor and outdoor storage areas
B. observed for indoor storage areas only
C. observed for outdoor storage areas only
D. eliminated for indoor and outdoor storage areas

KEY (CORRECT ANSWERS)

1.	D	11.	C	21.	B	31.	A	41.	B
2.	A	12.	A	22.	B	32.	C	42.	D
3.	A	13.	C	23.	D	33.	C	43.	C
4.	D	14.	B	24.	C	34.	D	44.	A
5.	C	15.	B	25.	B	35.	B	45.	B
6.	B	16.	B	26.	C	36.	D	46.	D
7.	D	17.	A	27.	B	37.	A	47.	D
8.	C	18.	C	28.	D	38.	C	48.	B
9.	A	19.	A	29.	B	39.	C	49.	B
10.	A	20.	A	30.	D	40.	D	50.	A

EXAMINATION SECTION
TEST 1

DIRECTIONS: Each question or incomplete statement is followed by several suggested answers or completions. Select the one that BEST answers the question or completes the statement. *PRINT THE LETTER OF THE CORRECT ANSWER IN THE SPACE AT THE RIGHT.*

1. Assume that your warehouse received a shipment of 600 articles. A sample of 60 articles was inspected. Of this sample, one article was wholly defective, and four articles were partly defective. On the basis of this sampling, you would expect the total number of defective articles in this shipment to be 1.____

   A. 5   B. 10   C. 40   D. 50

2. The stock inventory card for paint, white, flat, one gallon, has the following entries: 2.____

Date	Received	Shipped	Balance
April 12	-	25	75
April 13	50	75	
April 14	-	10	
April 15	25	-	
April 16	-	10	

   The balance on hand at the close of business on April 15 should be

   A. 40   B. 45   C. 55   D. 65

Questions 3-8.

DIRECTIONS: For each Question 3 through 8, select the choice whose meaning is MOST NEARLY the same as that of the numbered item.

3. ADJACENT 3.____

   A. near   B. critical   C. sensitive   D. sharp

4. CONSOLIDATE 4.____

   A. divide in half   B. direct
   C. agree   D. unite

5. DETERIORATE 5.____

   A. decorate   B. prevent   C. regulate   D. worsen

6. EXPEDITE 6.____

   A. label carefully   B. process promptly
   C. represent   D. terminate

7. NEGLIGENT 7.____

   A. careless   B. painful   C. pleasant   D. positive

8. VENDOR 8.____

   A. customer   B. inspector   C. manager   D. seller

Questions 9-12.

DIRECTIONS: Questions 9 through 12 are to be answered SOLELY on the basis of the following passage.

Several special factors must be taken into account in selecting trucks to be used in a warehouse that stores food in freezer and cold storage rooms. Since gasoline fumes may contaminate the food, the trucks should be powered by electricity, not by gasoline. The trucks must be specially equipped to operate in the extreme cold of freezer rooms. The equipment must be dependable, for if a truck breaks down while transporting frozen food from a railroad car to the freezer of a warehouse, this expensive merchandise will quickly spoil. Finally, since cold storage and freezer rooms are expensive to operate, commodities must be stored close together, and the aisles between the rows of commodities must be as narrow as possible. Therefore, the trucks must be designed to work even in narrow aisles.

9. Of the following, the BEST title for the above passage is: 9.___

   A. Expenses Involved in Operating a Freezer or Cold Storage Room
   B. How to Prevent Food Spoilage in Freezer and Cold Storage Rooms
   C. Selecting the Best Trucks to Use in a Food Storage Warehouse
   D. The Problem of Contamination of Food by Gasoline Fumes

10. According to the above passage, electrically powered trucks should be used for moving food in freezer and cold storage rooms chiefly because they 10.___

    A. are cheaper to operate than gasoline powered trucks
    B. are dependable
    C. can operate in extremes of heat and cold
    D. do not produce fumes which may contaminate food

11. Trucks designed for use in narrow aisles should be used in freezer and cold storage rooms because 11.___

    A. commodities are placed close together in freezer rooms to save space
    B. commodities spoil quickly if the space between aisles in the freezer is too wide
    C. narrow aisle trucks are more dependable
    D. narrow aisle trucks are run by electricity

12. According to the above passage, all of the following factors should be taken into account in selecting a truck for use to transport frozen food into and within a cold storage room EXCEPT 12.___

    A. ability to operate in extreme cold
    B. dependability
    C. the weight of the truck
    D. whether or not the truck emits exhaust fumes

Questions 13-22.

DIRECTIONS: For Questions 13 through 22, choose from the given classifications the one under which the item is MOST likely to be found in general stock catalogs.

13. *Columnar pads* may BEST be classified under 13.____

A. dry goods, textiles, and floor covering
B. hospital and surgical supplies
C. recreational supplies and equipment
D. stationery and office supplies

14. *Trowels* may BEST be classified under 14.____

A. dry goods and textiles
B. hand tools and agricultural implements
C. household supplies
D. surgical supplies

15. *Collanders* may BEST be classified under 15.____

A. building materials
B. kitchen utensils
C. motor vehicle parts
D. plumbing supplies

16. *Litmus paper* may BEST be classified under 16.____

A. laboratory supplies
B. sewing supplies
C. stationery and supplies
D. textiles

17. *Pipettes* may BEST be classified under 17.____

A. hardware
B. hospital and laboratory supplies
C. kitchen utensils and tableware
D. plumbing fixtures and parts

18. *Carbon tetrachloride* may BEST be classified under 18.____

A. brushes
B. clothing and textiles
C. drugs and chemicals
D. toilet articles and accessories

19. *Curry powder* may BEST be classified under 19.____

A. drugs and chemicals
B. food and condiments
C. paints and supplies
D. surgical and dental supplies

20. *Wing nuts* may BEST be classified under 20.____

A. food and condiments
B. hardware supplies
C. household utensils
D. sewing supplies

21. *Shears* may BEST be classified under 21.____

A. agricultural implements
B. clothing and textiles
C. electrical parts
D. furniture

22. *Chambray* may BEST be classified under 22.____

A. canned goods, food, and miscellaneous groceries
B. brooms and brushes
C. drugs and chemicals
D. dry goods and textiles

23. Four city-owned trucks, all the same make, model, and capacity, were dispatched on round trips each with a 120 gallon tank full of gas. After Truck A had traveled 225 miles, his tank was 1/4 full. After Truck B had traveled 120 miles, his tank was 1/2 full. After Truck C had traveled 75 miles, his tank was 3/4 full. After Truck D had traveled 300 miles, his tank was empty. Which truck had the POOREST average mileage per gallon of gas? Truck 23.____

A. A B. B C. C D. D

24. Assume that you receive a shipment of 9 boxes of paper towels. Each box contains 6 dozen packages. Each package contains 200 paper towels. The total cost of the shipment of boxes is $64.80. The unit of issue for paper towels is the package. The unit cost of the paper towels is 24.____

A. $0.10 B. $0.90 C. $1.20 D. $7.20

25. One shipment of 70 shovels costs $140. A second shipment of 130 shovels costs $208. The average cost per shovel for both shipments is MOST NEARLY 25.____

A. $1.60 B. $1.75 C. $2.00 D. $2.50

KEY (CORRECT ANSWERS)

1. D
2. D
3. A
4. D
5. D

6. B
7. A
8. D
9. C
10. D

11. A
12. C
13. D
14. B
15. B

16. A
17. B
18. C
19. B
20. B

21. A
22. D
23. B
24. A
25. B

TEST 2

DIRECTIONS: Each question or incomplete statement is followed by several suggested answers or completions. Select the one that BEST answers the question or completes the statement. *PRINT THE LETTER OF THE CORRECT ANSWER IN THE SPACE AT THE RIGHT.*

Questions 1-5.

DIRECTIONS: Questions 1 through 5 show items that have been requisitioned by city agencies. In each group of four items, there is one item which has NOT been described in sufficient detail to enable the storekeeper or his subordinates to fill the order promptly from the variety of stock on hand. For each question, select the item that has pertinent, important information missing.

1. A. Fuses, auto, glass, 25 volts 1.____
   B. Ladders, extension, 2 sections, 30', metal
   C. Paint, interior, white, 1 gallon can, flat
   D. Stoppers, rubber, solid, white, nickel plated, brass ring, 1"

2. A. Aspirin, U.S.P., 1 grain - 1,000 in bottle 2.____
   B. Blotters, desk, 120 lb. stock, 24" x 38", green
   C. Folders, file, manila, 1/3 cut
   D. Nutmeg, ground, 1 lb. container

3. A. Safety pins, brass, nickel plated, size 2 3.____
   B. Sheets, bed, cotton, white
   C. Thermometer, oven, 100/600 degree F, enamel
   D. Toothbrush, adult size, nylon bristle

4. A. Pencil, black lead, #2, general office use, with eraser 4.____
   B. Stencil, dry-process, blue, legal size #2960
   C. Tape, cellulose, 1/2 in. x 1296 in., core diameter 1 in.
   D. Typewriter ribbon, standard, black record

5. A. Fruits, canned, peaches 5.____
   B. Milk, processed, dry powdered, whole, bulk
   C. Olives, stuffed, 16 oz. bottle, 12 bottles to case
   D. Sugar, granulated, 100 lb. bag

6. The deterioration of some items is accelerated when temperature exceeds 70° F and humidity is greater than 40 percent. 6.____
   Of the following, the item that would be LEAST affected by increases of temperature and humidity above these amounts is

   A. bristle brushes
   B. cellophane tape
   C. rice
   D. typewriter ribbons

7. The storage life of many items varies according to temperature and humidity. 7.____
   To gain maximum storage life, the one of the following items which should be stored in an area having a temperature of 55° F with 50 percent relative humidity is

A. clothing
B. steel parts
C. tires
D. x-ray film

8. A shipment of 200 creosote logs 12" in diameter with lengths varying from 20' to 30' each will arrive on flatbed trucks and are to be stored. The mode of power to be employed to move the logs from the flatbeds to an outdoor storage area is a warehouse crane. To avoid slippage, the pulley ropes or chains should be attached to the logs with a 8.____

A. double basket sling
B. double choker sling with hooks attached
C. four leg bridle sling with spliced eyes
D. hammock sling

Questions 9-12.

DIRECTIONS: Questions 9 through 12 represent items appearing on requisitions received in a storehouse. Assume that you have a wide variety of each item named. Some important information is missing from each description. Without this missing information (NOT code number or account number), it would be difficult to select the appropriate item from the variety in stock. From the choices given, select the one that represents the missing additional information that would be MOST important and helpful in filling each requisition.

9. PAPER, mimeograph, 100% sulphite sub 20, white 9.____

A. bond or onionskin
B. ruled or unruled
C. size of paper
D. two or three holes

10. NEEDLES, hand sewing, 20 to package 10.____

A. cost
B. metallic composition
C. purpose
D. size

11. SCREWS, wood, gross in box, brass, 1/2", No. 2 11.____

A. round or flat head
B. size of bolt
C. type of lumber for which used
D. type of metal of which made

12. THREAD, SPOOL COTTON, hand sewing, 6 cord, 500 yd., one dozen in box, #60 12.____

A. color of thread
B. size of needle's eye
C. type of fabric to be sewn
D. diameter of spool

13. Of the following, the LEAST appropriate preservative to apply to a wooden ladder is 13.____

A. clear varnish
B. lacquer
C. linseed oil
D. paint

14. Of the following, the type of lighting that is MOST efficient for maximum illumination in an equipment maintenance area is 14.____

A. *incandescent* (direct)
B. *incandescent* (general diffusing)
C. *fluorescent* (direct)
D. *fluorescent* (semi-direct)

15. Of the following chemicals, the one which is MOST hazardous and requires extra precautionary storage and handling methods is 15.____

A. citric acid
B. hydrogen peroxide
C. nitric acid
D. oxalic acid

16. You are informed that several cases of canned condensed milk have spoiled and you are assigned to seek the cause and find a remedy. 16.____
In the absence of any specific information, which of the following is MOST likely to have been the cause of this spoilage?

A. Improper rotation of stock
B. Adequate ventilation
C. Insect infestation
D. Insufficient heat

17. Inventory records are essential to efficient warehouse operations. 17.____
Of the following purposes served by inventory records, the one which is of LEAST importance to warehouse operating personnel is the

A. establishment of quantity controls
B. estimation of present values of items
C. identification of stock items
D. location of stock items

18. When in storage, the one of the following which it is MOST important to sprinkle periodically with naphthalene flakes is 18.____

A. canvas cots
B. cotton towels
C. manila rope
D. wool blankets

19. Generally, the time required to fill a requisition will be LEAST affected by the ______ of the item requisitioned. 19.____

A. amount
B. dimensions
C. length of the description
D. location

20. Of the following, the BEST procedure to follow in order to insure that a laborer has understood instructions that you have just given to him is to 20.____

A. ask the laborer if he has any questions about the instructions
B. have the laborer explain the instructions to you
C. repeat the key points of the instructions to the laborer
D. write out the instructions and give them to the laborer

21. You have been assigned several newly-appointed inexperienced stockmen and laborers whose performance in inadequate. 21.____
Of the following, the BEST course of action is to

A. commence a training program for all employees under your supervision
B. provide special guidance to those employees whose performance is inadequate
C. do a work simplification study
D. take steps to improve morale through incentive awards

22. Assume that one of your subordinates knows more about a certain aspect of the work than you do. You notice that many of the workers go to him rather than to you for advice on this aspect of the work. 22.____
You should

A. delegate your authority and responsibility in this aspect of the work to this subordinate
B. direct the workers to bring all questions about the work to you
C. permit this to continue as long as it does not interfere with the work of this subordinate
D. tell this subordinate that he is to refer any requests for information to you

23. Assume that about 11 A.M. one of your stockmen reports to you that one of the assistant stockmen appears to be drunk and is creating a disturbance in the warehouse. The MOST appropriate action for you to take FIRST in this situation is to 23.____

A. ask the stockman to bring the assistant stockman who appears to be drunk to your office
B. call the police department for assistance
C. go with the stockman to investigate the matter
D. report the matter to your supervisor

24. Assume that you have received an anonymous letter alleging that the crew of one of your delivery trucks has been observed parked at a certain location for periods of one hour or more on several occasions. This location is not in the vicinity of any agency where your crew would be required to make deliveries. 24.____
In this situation, the MOST appropriate action for you to take is to

A. break up the crew by reassigning each member to other duties
B. follow the crew for several days as they are making deliveries
C. ignore the letter since it is anonymous
D. interview each member of the crew privately to find out what he has to say about the allegation

25. Assume that one of your subordinates has gotten into the habit of regularly and routinely referring every small problem which arises in his work to you. 25.____
In order to help him overcome this habit, it is generally MOST advisable for you to

A. advise him that you do not have time to discuss each problem with him and that he should do whatever he wants
B. ask your subordinate for his solution and approve any satisfactory approach that he suggests
C. refuse to discuss such routine problems with him
D. tell him that he should consider looking for another position if he does not feel competent to solve such routine problems

---

KEY (CORRECT ANSWERS)

1. A
2. C
3. B
4. D
5. A

6. A
7. D
8. B
9. C
10. D

11. A
12. A
13. D
14. C
15. C

16. A
17. B
18. D
19. C
20. B

21. B
22. C
23. C
24. D
25. B

EXAMINATION SECTION
TEST 1

DIRECTIONS: Each question or incomplete statement is followed by several suggested answers or completions. Select the one that BEST answers the question or completes the statement. *PRINT THE LETTER OF THE CORRECT ANSWER IN THE SPACE AT THE RIGHT.*

1. The process of determining the quantity of goods and materials that are in stock is commonly called 1.____

   A. receiving
   B. disbursement
   C. reconciliation
   D. inventory

2. Proper and effective storage procedure involves the storing of 2.____

   A. items together on the basis of class grouping
   B. all items in chronological order based on date received
   C. items in alphabetical order based on date of delivery
   D. items randomly wherever space is available

3. Which of the following is the FIRST step involved in correctly taking an inventory? 3.____

   A. Reconciliation of inventory records with the number of items on hand
   B. Analysis of possible discrepancies between items on hand and the stock record balance
   C. Identification and recording of the locations of all items in stock
   D. Issuance of an inventory directive to all vendors

4. Supply items other than food which are subject to deterioration should be checked 4.____

   A. at delivery time only
   B. occasionally
   C. only when issued
   D. periodically

5. For which of the following supplies is it MOST necessary to provide ample ventilation? 5.____

   A. Small rubber parts
   B. Metal products
   C. Flammable liquids
   D. Wooden items

6. Storing small lots of supplies in an area designated for the storage of large lots of supplies will generally result in 6.____

   A. *loss* of supplies
   B. *loss* of storage space
   C. *increase* in inventory
   D. *increase* in storage space

7. Compliance with fire preventive measures is a major requirement for the maintenance of a safe warehouse. Which of the following statements is LEAST important in describing a measure useful in maintaining a fire preventive facility? 7.____

   A. Smoking is only permitted in designated areas.
   B. Oil-soaked rags should be disposed of promptly and not stored.
   C. When not in use, electrical machinery should be grounded.
   D. Gasoline-powered materials handling equipment should not be refueled with the motor running.

8. It is POOR storage practice to store small valuable items loosely in open containers in bulk storage areas because doing so results in the 8.____

   A. misplacement of such items
   B. pilferage of these items
   C. deterioration of such supplies
   D. hindrance in inspection of these supplies

9. Assume that you have been placed in charge of the receiving operations at your garage. Generally, you receive all the supplies you order during the first week of each month. Of the following, the MOST effective and economic way to facilitate receiving operations would be to 9.____

   A. secure overtime authorization for laborers during that week
   B. have all truck deliveries made in one day
   C. stagger truck deliveries throughout each morning of the week
   D. assign all personnel to receiving duty for that week

10. Effective security measures must be instituted to provide for the safekeeping of city supplies.
However, the scope and complexity of security measures used at a warehouse facility should correspond MOST NEARLY to the 10.____

   A. value of supplies stored in the warehouse
   B. borough in which the warehouse is located
   C. level of warehouse activity
   D. age of the warehouse facility

11. To facilitate handling and issuance of supply items that have a high turnover rate, they should generally be stored 11.____

   A. away from accessible aisles
   B. on upper shelves
   C. in a locked compartment area
   D. close to the service counter area

12. The MOST important factor to be considered in effectively storing heavy, bulky, and difficult-to-handle items is to store these items 12.____

   A. as close to shipping areas as possible
   B. in storage areas with a low floor-load capacity
   C. only in outside storage sheds
   D. away from aisles

Questions 13-16.

DIRECTIONS: Questions 13 through 16 are to be answered using ONLY the information in the following passage.

Fire exit drills should be established and held periodically to effectively train personnel to leave their working area promptly upon proper signal and to evacuate the building speedily but without confusion. All fire exit drills should be carefully planned and carried out in a serious manner under rigid discipline so as to provide positive protection in the event of a real emergency. As a general rule, the local fire department should be furnished advance information regarding the exact date and time the exit drill is scheduled. When it is impossible to hold regular drills, written instructions should be distributed to all employees.

Depending upon individual circumstances, fires in warehouses vary from those of fast development that are almost instantly beyond any possibility of employee control to others of relatively slow development where a small readily attackable flame may be present for periods of time up to 15 minutes or more during which simple attack with fire extinguishers or small building hoses may prevent the fire development. In any case, it is characteristic of many warehouse fires that at a certain point in development they flash up to the top of the stack, increase heat quickly, and spread rapidly. There is a degree of inherent danger in attacking warehouse type fires and all employees should be thoroughly trained in the use of the types of extinguishers or small hoses in the buildings and well instructed in the necessity of always staying between the fire and a direct pass to an exit.

13. Employees should be instructed that, when fighting a fire, they MUST 13.____

    A. try to control the blaze
    B. extinguish any fire in 15 minutes
    C. remain between the fire and a direct passage to the exit
    D. keep the fire between themselves and the fire exit

14. Whenever conditions are such that regular fire drills cannot be held, then which one of the following actions should be taken? 14.____

    A. The local fire department should be notified.
    B. Rigid discipline should be maintained during work hours.
    C. Personnel should be instructed to leave their working area by whatever means are available.
    D. Employees should receive fire drill procedures in writing.

15. The passage indicates that the purpose of fire exit drills is to train employees to 15.____

    A. control a fire before it becomes uncontrollable
    B. act as firefighters
    C. leave the working area promptly
    D. be serious

16. According to the passage, fire exit drills will prove to be of *utmost* effectiveness if 16.____

    A. employee participation is made voluntary
    B. they take place periodically
    C. the fire department actively participates
    D. they are held without advance planning

Questions 17-20.

DIRECTIONS: Questions 17 through 20 are to be answered using ONLY the information in the following paragraph.

A report is frequently ineffective because the person writing it is not fully acquainted with all the necessary details before he actually starts to construct the report. All details pertaining to the subject should be known before the report is started. If the essential facts are not known, they should be investigated. It is wise to have essential facts written down rather than to depend too much on memory, especially if the facts pertain to such matters as amounts, dates, names of persons, or other specific data. When the necessary information has been gathered, the general plan and content of the report should be thought out before the writing is actually begun. A person with little or no experience in writing reports may find that it is wise to make a brief outline. Persons with more experience should not need a written outline, but they should make mental notes of the steps they are to follow. If writing reports without dictation is a regular part of an office worker's duties, he should set aside a certain time during the day when he is least likely to be interrupted. That may be difficult, but in most offices there are certain times in the day when the callers, telephone calls, and other interruptions are not numerous. During those times, it is best to write reports that need undivided concentration. Reports that are written amid a series of interruptions may be poorly done.

17. Before starting to write an effective report, it is necessary to 17.____

    A. memorize all specific information
    B. disregard ambiguous data
    C. know all pertinent information
    D. develop a general plan

18. Reports dealing with complex and difficult material should be 18.____

    A. prepared and written by the supervisor of the unit
    B. written when there is the least chance of interruption
    C. prepared and written as part of regular office routine
    D. outlined and then dictated

19. According to the passage, employees with no prior familiarity in writing reports may find it helpful to 19.____

    A. prepare a brief outline
    B. mentally prepare a synopsis of the report's content
    C. have a fellow employee help in writing the report
    D. consult previous reports

20. In writing a report, needed information which is unclear should be 20.____

    A. disregarded
    B. investigated
    C. memorized
    D. gathered

KEY (CORRECT ANSWERS)

1.	D	11.	D
2.	A	12.	A
3.	C	13.	C
4.	D	14.	D
5.	C	15.	C
6.	B	16.	B
7.	C	17.	C
8.	B	18.	B
9.	C	19.	A
10.	A	20.	B

TEST 2

DIRECTIONS: Each question or incomplete statement is followed by several suggested answers or completions. Select the one that BEST answers the question or completes the statement. *PRINT THE LETTER OF THE CORRECT ANSWER IN THE SPACE AT THE RIGHT.*

Questions 1-4.

DIRECTIONS: Questions 1 through 4 are to be answered using ONLY the information in the following passage.

The operation and maintenance of the stock-location system is a warehousing function and responsibility. The stock locator system shall consist of a file of stock-location record cards, either manually or mechanically prepared, depending upon the equipment available. The file shall contain an individual card for each stock item stored in the depot, with the records maintained in stock number sequence.

The locator file is used for all receiving, warehousing, inventory, and shipping activities in the depot. The locator file must contain complete and accurate data to provide ready support to the various depot functions and activities, i.e., processing shipping documents, updating records on mechanized equipment, where applicable, supplying accurate locator information for stock selection and proper storage of receipts, consolidating storage locations of identical items not subject to shelf-life control, and preventing the consolidation of stock of limited shelf-life items. The file is also essential in accomplishing location surveys and the inventory program.

Storage of bulk stock items by "spot-location" method is generally recognized as the best means of obtaining maximum warehouse space utilization. Despite the fact that the spot-location method of storage enables full utilization of storage capacity, this method may prove inefficient unless it is supplemented by adequate stock-location control, including proper lay-out and accurate maintenance of stock locator cards.

1. The manner in which the stock-location record cards should be filed is 1.____

   A. alphabetically B. chronologically
   C. numerically D. randomly

2. Items of limited shelf-life should 2.____

   A. not be stored
   B. not be stored together
   C. be stored in stock sequence
   D. be stored together

3. Which one of the following is NOT mentioned in the passage as a use of the stock-location system? 3.____
   Aids in

   A. accomplishing location surveys
   B. providing information for stock selection
   C. storing items received for the first time
   D. processing shipping documents

4. If the spot-location method of storing is used, then the use of the stock-location system is 4.____

   A. *desirable,* because the stock-location system is recognized as the best means of obtaining maximum warehouse space utilization
   B. *undesirable,* because additional records must be kept
   C. *desirable,* because stock-location controls are necessary with the spot-location storage method
   D. *undesirable,* because a stock-locator system will take up valuable storage space

Questions 5-8.

DIRECTIONS: Questions 5 through 8 are to be answered using ONLY the information in the following paragraph.

Known damage is defined as damage that is apparent and acknowledged by the carrier at the time of delivery to the purchaser. A meticulous inspection of the damaged goods should be completed by the purchaser and a notation specifying the extent of the damage should be applied to the carrier's original freight bill. As is the case in known loss, it is necessary for the carrier's agent to acknowledge by signature the damage notation in order for it to have any legal status. The purchaser should not refuse damaged freight since it is his legal duty to accept the property and to employ every available and reasonable means to protect the shipment and minimize the loss. Acceptance of a damaged shipment does not endanger any legitimate claim the purchaser may have against the carrier for damage. If the purchaser fails to observe the legal duty to accept damaged freight, the carrier may consider it abandoned. After properly notifying the vendor and purchaser of his intentions, the carrier may dispose of the material at public sale.

5. Before disposing of an abandoned shipment, the carrier must 5.____

   A. notify the vendor and the carrier's agent
   B. advise the vendor and purchaser of his plans
   C. notify the purchaser and the carrier's agent
   D. obtain the signature of the carrier's agent on the freight bill

6. In the case of damaged freight, the original freight bill will only have legal value if it is signed by the 6.____

   A. carrier's agent
   B. purchaser
   C. vendor
   D. purchaser and vendor

7. A purchaser does not protect a shipment of cargo that is damaged and is further deteriorating. 7.____
   According to the above paragraph, the action of the purchaser is

   A. *acceptable,* because he is not obligated to protect damaged cargo
   B. *unacceptable,* because damaged cargo must be protected no matter what is involved
   C. *acceptable,* because he took possession of the cargo
   D. *unacceptable,* because he is obligated by law to protect the cargo

8. The TWO requirements that must be satisfied before cargo can be labeled *known damage* are signs of evident damage and 8.____

A. confirmation by the carrier or carrier's agent that this is so
B. delayed shipment of goods
C. signature of acceptance by the purchaser
D. acknowledgment by the vendor that this is so

Questions 9-13.

DIRECTIONS: Questions 9 through 13 are to be answered on the basis of the following graph.

GARBAGE COLLECTIONS MADE JAN. 1 - DEC. 31, IN TONS (SHORT TON)

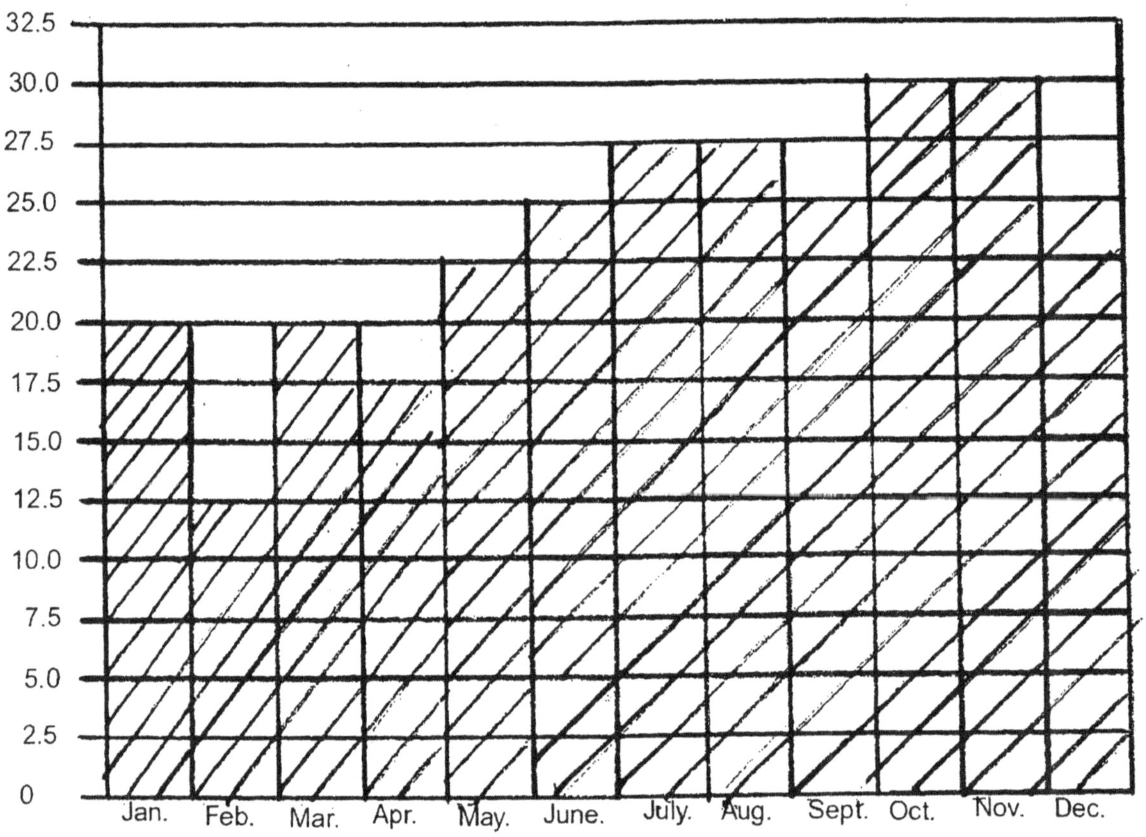

9. According to the information presented in the graph, the weight of the average monthly collection of garbage is MOST NEARLY ______ tons. 9.____

A. 22.5 B. 23.5 C. 24.5 D. 25.5

10. If a truck can carry 6,000 lbs., then the number of truck-loads collected during the year was MOST NEARLY 10.____

A. 55 B. 75 C. 95 D. 115

11. The amount of garbage collected during the second half of the year represents APPROXIMATELY what percentage of the total garbage collected during the year? 11.____

A. 50% B. 60% C. 70% D. 80%

12. During the months of September, October, and November, approximately 12% of the collections consisted of fallen leaves. 12.____
What was the weight of the remaining garbage NOT containing fallen leaves for that period?
_______ tons.

A. 10 B. 20 C. 65 D. 75

13. Assume that the collections for the year as shown in the above graph exceeded the previous year's collection by 17%. The collection made in the previous year was MOST NEARLY _______ tons. 13.____

A. 50 B. 225 C. 240 D. 275

Questions 14-17.

DIRECTIONS: Questions 14 through 17 are to be answered on the basis of the following graph

INVENTORY LEVELS (IN DOZENS) OF ITEM A IN STOREHOUSE
AT BEGINNING OF MONTH FOR A PERIOD OF TWELVS MONTH

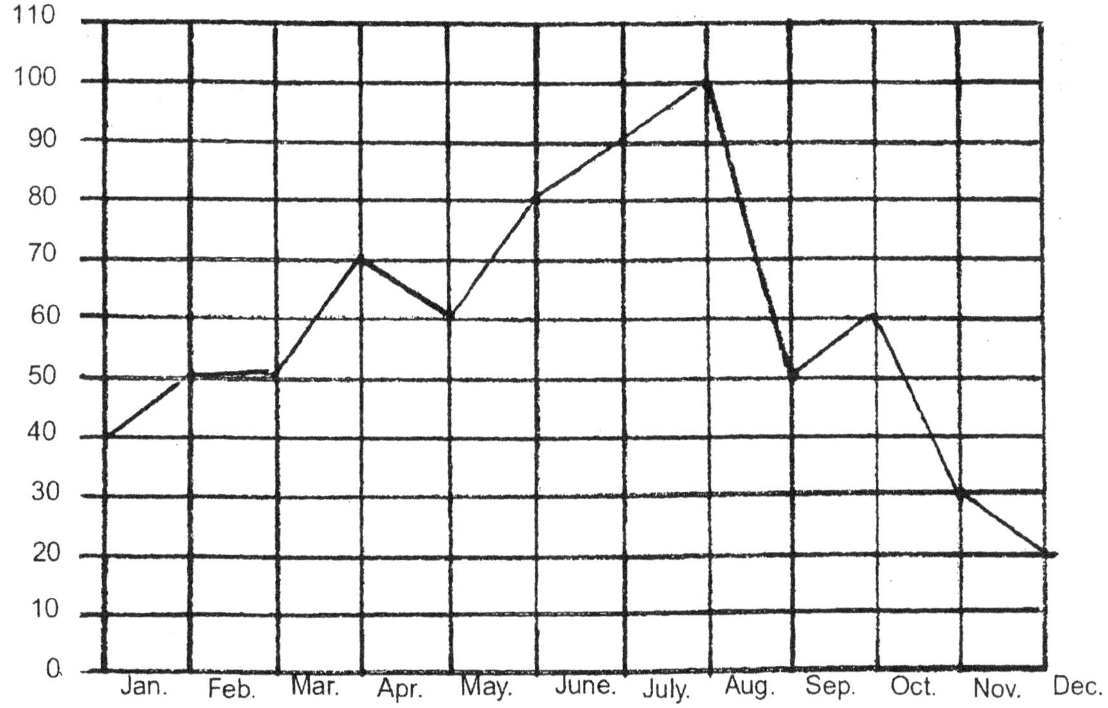

14. The average monthly inventory level during the course of the year was MOST NEARLY _______ dozen. 14.____

A. 45 B. 60 C. 75 D. 90

15. If one dozen items fit in a carton measuring 2 feet by 2 feet by 3 feet, what MINIMUM volume would be required to store the maximum August inventory? 15.____
_______ cubic feet.

A. 12 B. 100 C. 700 D. 1,200

16. Assume that deliveries are made to the storehouse on the first working day of each month. If 30% of the June inventory was consumed during the month, how many items had to be delivered to reach the July inventory level? 16.____
______ items.

A. 288 B. 408 C. 696 D. 1,080

17. Which three-month period contained the LOWEST average inventory level? 17.____

A. Jan., Feb., March
B. April, May, June
C. July, Aug., Sept.
D. Oct., Nov., Dec.

18. Assume that it takes approximately 1 1/2 minutes to unload a dozen identical items from a delivery truck. 18.____
At this speed, the amount of time it should take to unload a shipment of 876 items is MOST NEARLY ______ minutes.

A. 90 B. 100 C. 110 D. 120

19. Assume that a shop clerk has received a bill of $108 for a delivery of clamps which cost $4.32 per dozen. 19.____
How many clamps should there be in this delivery?

A. 25 B. 36 C. 300 D. 360

20. Employee A has not used any leave time and has accumulated a total of 45 leave days. How many months did it take Employee A to have accumulated 45 leave days if the accrual rate is 1 2/3 days per month? 20.____

A. 25 B. 27 C. 29 D. 31

KEY (CORRECT ANSWERS)

1.	C	11.	B
2.	B	12.	D
3.	C	13.	C
4.	C	14.	B
5.	B	15.	D
6.	A	16.	B
7.	D	17.	D
8.	A	18.	C
9.	B	19.	C
10.	C	20.	B

EXAMINATION SECTION
TEST 1

DIRECTIONS: Each question or incomplete statement is followed by several suggested answers or completions. Select the one that BEST answers the question or completes the statement. *PRINT THE LETTER OF THE CORRECT ANSWER IN THE SPACE AT THE RIGHT.*

1. A shop clerk is notified that only 75 bolts can be supplied by Vendor A. 1.____
If this represents 12.5% of the total requisition, then how many bolts were *originally* ordered?

A. 125 B. 600 C. 700 D. 900

2. An enclosed square-shaped storage area with sides of 16 feet each has a safe-load capacity of 250 pounds per square foot. 2.____
The MAXIMUM evenly distributed weight that can be stored in this area is ______ lbs.

A. 1,056 B. 4,000 C. 64,000 D. 102,400

3. A clerical employee has completed 70 progress reports the first week, 87 the second week, and 80 the third week. Assuming a 4-week month, how many progress reports must the clerk complete in the fourth week in order to attain an average of 85 progress reports per week for the month? 3.____

A. 93 B. 103 C. 113 D. 133

4. On the first of the month, Shop X received a delivery of 150 gallons of lubricating oil. During the month, the following amounts of oil were used on lubricating work each week: 30 quarts, 36 quarts, 20 quarts, and 48 quarts. The amount of lubricating oil *remaining* at the end of the month was ______ gallons. 4.____

A. 4 B. 33.5 C. 41.5 D. 116.5

5. For working a 35-hour week, Employee A earns a gross amount of $480.90. For each hour that Employee A works over 40 hours a week, he is entitled to 1 1/2 times his hourly wage rate. 5.____
If Employee A worked 9 hours on Monday, 8 hours on Tuesday, 9 hours 30 minutes on Wednesday, 9 hours 15 minutes on Thursday, and 9 hours 15 minutes on Friday, what should his *gross* salary be for that week?

A. $618.30 B. $632.04 C. $652.65 D. $687.00

6. An enclosed cube-shaped storage bay has dimensions of 12 feet by 12 feet by 12 feet. Standard procedure requires that there be at least 1 foot of space between the walls, the ceiling, and the stored items. 6.____
What is the MAXIMUM number of cube-shaped boxes with length, width, and height of 1 foot each that can be stored on 1-foot high pallets in this bay?

A. 1,000 B. 1,331 C. 1,452 D. 1,728

7. Assume that two ceilings are to be painted. One ceiling measures 30 feet by 15 feet and the second 45 feet by 60 feet. 7.____
If one quart of paint will cover 60 square feet of ceiling, *approximately* how much paint will be required to paint the two ceilings? ______ gallons.

A. 6 B. 10 C. 13 D. 18

8. In last year's budget, $7,500 was spent for office supplies. Of this amount, 60% was spent for paper supplies. If the price of paper has risen 20% over last year's price, then the amount that will be spent this year on paper supplies, assuming the same quantity will be purchased, will be 8.___

A. $3,600 B. $5,200 C. $5,400 D. $6,000

Questions 9-13.

DIRECTIONS: Questions 9 through 13 are to be answered on the basis of the following information.

A certain shop keeps an informational card file on all suppliers and merchandise. On each card is the supplier's name, the contrast number for the merchandise he supplies, and a delivery date for the merchandise. In this filing system, the supplier's name is filed alphabetically, the contract number for the merchandise is filed numerically, and the delivery date is filed chronologically.

In Questions 9 through 13, there are five notations numbered 1 through 5 shown in Column I. Each notation is made up of a supplier's name, a contract number, and a date which is to be filed according to the following rules:

First: *File in alphabetical order*
Second: *When two or more notations have the same supplier, file according to the contract number in numerical order beginning with the lowest number*
Third: *When two or more notations have the same supplier and contract number, file according to the date beginning with the earliest date.*

In Column II, the numbers 1 through 5 are arranged in four ways to show four different orders in which the merchandise information might be filed. Pick the answer (A, B, C, or D) in Column II in which the notations are arranged according to the above filing rules.

SAMPLE QUESTION:

COLUMN I	*COLUMN II*
1. *Cluney (4865) 6/17/05*	A. *2, 3, 4, 1, 5*
2. *Roster (2466) 5/10/04*	B. *2, 5, 1, 3, 4*
3. *Altool (7114) 10/15/05*	C. *3, 2, 1, 4, 5*
4. *Cluney (5276) 12/18/04*	D. *3, 5, 1, 4, 2*
5. *Cluney (4865) 4/8/05*	

The CORRECT way to file the cards is:

3. Altool (7114) 10/15/05
5. Cluney (4865) 4/8/05
1. Cluney (4865) 6/17/05
4. Cluney (5276) 12/18/04
2. Roster (2466) 5/10/04

Since the correct filing order is 3, 5, 1, 4, 2, the answer to the sample question is D.

	COLUMN I	COLUMN II	
9.	1. Warren (96063) 3/30/06	A. 2, 4, 3, 5, 1	9.____
	2. Moore (21237) 9/4/07	B. 2, 3, 5, 4, 1	
	3. Newman (10050) 12/12/06	C. 4, 5, 2, 3, 1	
	4. Downs (81251) 1/2/06	D. 4, 2, 3, 5, 1	
	5. Oliver (60145) 6/30/07		
10.	1. Henry (40552) 7/6/07	A. 5, 4, 3, 1, 2	10.____
	2. Boyd (91251) 9/1/06	B. 2, 3, 4, 1, 5	
	3. George (8196) 12/12/06	C. 2, 4, 3, 1, 5	
	4. George (31096) 1/12/07	D. 5, 2, 3, 1, 4	
	5. West (6109) 8/9/06		
11.	1. Salba (4670) 9/7/06	A. 5, 3, 1, 2, 4	11.____
	2. Salba (51219) 3/1/06	B. 3, 1, 2, 4, 5	
	3. Crete (81562) 7/1/07	C. 3, 5, 4, 2, 1	
	4. Salba (51219) 1/11/07	D. 5, 3, 4, 2, 1	
	5. Texi (31549) 1/25/06		
12.	1. Crayone (87105) 6/10/07	A. 1, 2, 5, 3, 4	12.____
	2. Shamba (49210) 1/5/06	B. 1, 5, 2, 3, 4	
	3. Valiant (3152) 5/1/07	C. 1, 5, 3, 4, 2	
	4. Valiant (3152) 1/9/07	D. 1, 5, 2, 4, 3	
	5. Poro (59613) 7/1/06		
13.	1. Mackie (42169) 12/20/06	A. 3, 2, 1, 5, 4	13.____
	2. Lebo (5198) 9/12/05	B. 3, 2, 4, 5, 1	
	3. Drummon (99631) 9/9/07	C. 3, 5, 2, 4, 1	
	4. Lebo (15311) 1/25/05	D. 3, 5, 4, 2, 1	
	5. Harvin (81765) 6/2/06		

Questions 14-18.

DIRECTIONS: Questions 14 through 18 are to be answered on the basis of the following information.

In order to make sure stock is properly located, incoming units are stored as follows:

Stock Numbers	Bin Numbers
00100 - 39999	D30, L44
40000 - 69999	I4L, D38
70000 - 99999	41L, 80D
100000 and over	614, 83D

Using the above table, choose the answer (A, B, C, or D) which lists the correct bin number for the stock number given.

14. 17243 14.___

A. 41L B. 83D C. I4L D. D30

15. 9219 15.___

A. D38 B. L44 C. 614 D. 41L

16. 90125 16.___

A. 41L B. 614 C. D38 D. D30

17. 10001 17.___

A. L44 B. D38 C. SOD D. 83D

18. 200100 18.___

A. 41L B. I4L C. 83D D. D30

19. A supervisor believes that the current filing systems used in his office are not efficient. When his superior goes on vacation, he intends to change all the filing procedures. For a supervisor to undertake this move without his superior's knowledge would GENERALLY be considered 19.___

A. *advisable;* it shows that he has initiative
B. *Inadvisable,* the current filing systems are probably the best
C. *advisable;* the result will be an increase in productivity
D. *inadvisable;* the supervisor should be informed of any intended changes

20. Assume that you have been assigned the task of handling all telephone calls at a sanitation garage. After a recent snowstorm, your supervisor informed you that all available personnel have been assigned to snow removal duties. However, you have been receiving numerous telephone calls from the public in regard to unshoveled streets and intersections. 20.___
In handling these calls, it is generally considered good policy by the department to

A. indicate to the callers that the department is clearing streets off as quickly as possible
B. tell the callers there is nothing that can be done
C. tell the callers that they are tying up departmental telephones with needless complaints
D. promise the callers that streets will be cleared by the evening

KEY (CORRECT ANSWERS)

1. B
2. C
3. B
4. D
5. C

6. A
7. C
8. C
9. D
10. B

11. B
12. D
13. C
14. D
15. B

16. A
17. A
18. C
19. D
20. A

TEST 2

DIRECTIONS: Each question or incomplete statement is followed by several suggested answers or completions. Select the one that BEST answers the question or completes the statement. *PRINT THE LETTER OF TEE CORRECT ANSWER IN THE SPACE AT THE RIGHT.*

Questions 1-10.

DIRECTIONS: Questions 1 through 10 are to be answered on the basis of the following information.

A code number for any item is obtained by combining the date of delivery, number of units received, and number of units used.

The first two digits represent the day of the month, the third and fourth digits represent the month, and the fifth and sixth digits represent the year.

The number following the letter R represents the number of units received and the number following the letter U represents the number of units used.

For example, the code number 120673-R5690-U1001 indicates that a delivery of 5,690 units was made on June 12, of which 1,001 units were used.

Using the chart below, answer Questions 1 through 6 by choosing the letter (A, B, C, or D) in which the supplier and stock number correspond to the code number given.

Supplier	Stock Number	Number of Units Received	Delivery Date	Number of Units Used
Stony	38390	8300	May 11	3800
Stoney	39803	1780	September 15	1703
Nievo	21220	5527	October 10	5007
Nieve	38903	1733	August 5	1703
Monte	39213	5527	October 10	5007
Stony	38890	3308	December 9	3300
Stony	83930	3880	September 12	380
Nevo	47101	485	June 11	231
Nievo	12122	5725	May 11	5201
Neve	47101	9721	August 15	8207
Nievo	21120	2275	January 7	2175
Rosa	41210	3821	March 3	2710
Stony	38890	3308	September 12	3300
Dinal	54921	1711	April 2	1117
Stony	33890	8038	March 5	3300
Dinal	54721	1171	March 2	717
Claridge	81927	3308	April 5	3088
Nievo	21122	4878	June 7	3492
Haley	39670	8300	December 23	5300

1. Code No. 120972-R3308-U3300 1.____

   A. Nievo - 12122
   B. Stony - 83930
   C. Nievo - 21220
   D. Stony - 38890

2. Code No. 101072-R5527-U5007 2.____

A. Nievo - 21220
B. Haley - 39670
C. Monte - 39213
D. Claridge - 81927

3. Code No. 101073-R5527-U5007 3.____

A. Nievo - 21220
B. Monte - 39213
C. Nievo - 12122
D. Nievo - 21120

4. Code No. 110573-R5725-U5201 4.____

A. Nievo - 12122
B. Nievo - 21220
C. Haley - 39670
D. Stony - 38390

5. Code No. 070172-R2275-U2175 5.____

A. Stony - 33890
B. Stony - 83930
C. Stony - 38390
D. Nievo - 21120

6. Code No. 120972-R3880-U380 6.____

A. Stony - 83930
B. Stony - 38890
C. Stony - 33890
D. Monte - 39213

Using the same chart, answer Questions 7 through 10, choosing the letter (A, B, C, or D) in which the code number corresponds to the supplier and stock number given.

7. Nieve - 38903 7.____

A. 951973-R1733-U1703
B. 080572-R1733-U1703
C. 080573-R1733-U1703
D. 050873-R1733-U1703

8. Nevo - 47101 8.____

A. 081573-R9721-U8207
B. 091573-R9721-U8207]
C. 110672-R485-U231
D. 061172-R485-U231

9. Dinal - 54921 9.____

A. 020473-R1711-U1117
B. 030272-R1171-U717
C. 020372-R1171-U717
D. 421973-R1711-U1117

10. Nievo - 21122 10.____

A. 070672-R4878-U3492
B. 060772-R4878-U349
C. 761972-R4878-U3492
D. 060772-R4878-U3492

11. A citizen who has called the office at which you are working has started yelling on the telephone. He is annoyed because he has been switched from office to office and still has not reached the proper party. 11.____
Of the following, the BEST practice to follow is to

A. hang up on this individual since he is obviously a troublemaker
B. yell back at him for being so childish
C. tell him that you have heard that complaint before
D. try to calm this person and help him reach the proper party

12. Which of the following is the MOST likely result of employees publicly criticizing the activities of their agency? 12.____
The

A. employees will be terminated for the good of the agency
B. public's respect for the agency may decrease
C. productive members of the agency may resign
D. agency may sue these employees for libel

13. It is essential for city employees who deal with the public to provide service as promptly and completely as possible. 13.____
Letters from the public lodging complaints regarding poor service should GENERALLY be handled by

A. answering them as soon as possible according to agency procedures
B. ignoring them, since only troublemakers usually write such letters
C. returning them, since the city government does not respond to public complaints
D. acknowledging them with no further action necessary

14. While checking the work of a clerk who is under your supervision, you notice that he has made the same mistake a number of times. 14.____
In order to help prevent this clerk from making the same mistake again, it would be BEST for you to take which of the following courses of action?

A. Correct the errors yourself and not mention it to the clerk
B. Provide training for the clerk
C. Reprimand the clerk for the mistakes made
D. Remind the clerk of the errors he has previously made

15. A community resident calls the sanitation garage in which you are working to inquire about the days in which old furniture can be put on the street for collection. Although your unit is responsible for these collections, you do not have this information and there is nobody in the office to assist you. 15.____
Of the following, it would be MOST advisable to

A. tell the citizen to call back in an hour
B. get the citizen's telephone number and inform him that you will call back when you get the information
C. switch the call to another unit and let them get the information
D. put the caller on hold and try to find someone that has the answer

16. As a supervisor, you have been given the responsibility of maintaining attendance records for your garage. A co-worker, who has been late a number of times, has asked you to overlook his recent lateness since it involves only ten minutes. He has been warned previously for lateness and will receive some kind of disciplinary action because of this recent lateness, for you to overlook the lateness would be 16.____

A. *advisable;* it involves only a matter of ten minutes
B. *inadvisable;* this employee should have to suffer the consequences of his actions
C. *advisable;* morale in the unit will improve
D. *inadvisable;* employee lateness should never be excused

17. When a supervisor answers incoming telephone calls, it is important for him to FIRST 17.____

A. identify himself and/or his office
B. ask the caller to state the reason for the call
C. ask the caller the nature of the call
D. ask the caller to identify himself

18. It appears to you that the current mail distribution procedures are inefficient. 18.____
For you to make a suggestion to your supervisor for the implementation of new procedures, would be

A. *advisable;* if the supervisor thinks your ideas are worthwhile;they may be implemented
B. *inadvisable;* supervisors generally are not interested in changing procedures
C. *advisable;* new procedures generally provide better results than old procedures
D. *inadvisable;* only methods analysts should suggest changes in procedures

19. As a supervisor, you direct the work of two clerks. Recently, you discovered that one of the two clerks generally loafs around on Friday afternoons. This past Friday, you saw this particular employee standing around conversing with several employees. At that point, you severely reprimanded this employee in the presence of the other employees. 19.____
For you to have reprimanded this employee in such a fashion was

A. *advisable;* this employee *had it coming*
B. *inadvisable;* you should have spoken to him privately
C. *advisable;* this reprimand also served as a warning to the others
D. *inadvisable;* employees should not be reprimanded

20. As a supervisor, you have been assigned to maintain garage supplies. Recently, a co-worker requested a quantity of nails and screws for use in his home. Since this involves only a small amount of supplies, he felt it would not be wrong to make such a request. 20.____
In this case, it would be ADVISABLE for you to

A. give the co-worker the supplies
B. remind the co-worker that city supplies are only for city use
C. notify the investigation department in regard to this employee
D. forget the incident

KEY (CORRECT ANSWERS)

1.	D	11.	D
2.	C	12.	B
3.	A	13.	A
4.	A	14.	B
5.	D	15.	B
6.	A	16.	B
7.	D	17.	A
8.	C	18.	A
9.	A	19.	B
10.	A	20.	B

MECHANICAL APTITUDE
TOOLS AND THEIR USE

EXAMINATION SECTION

TEST 1

DIRECTIONS: Each question or incomplete statement is followed by several suggested answers or completions. Select the one that BEST answers the question or completes the statement. *PRINT THE LETTER OF THE CORRECT ANSWER IN THE SPACE AT THE RIGHT.*

Questions 1-15.

DIRECTIONS: Questions 1 through 15 refer to the tools shown below. The numbers in the answers refer to the numbers beneath the tools. NOTE: These tools are NOT shown to scale.

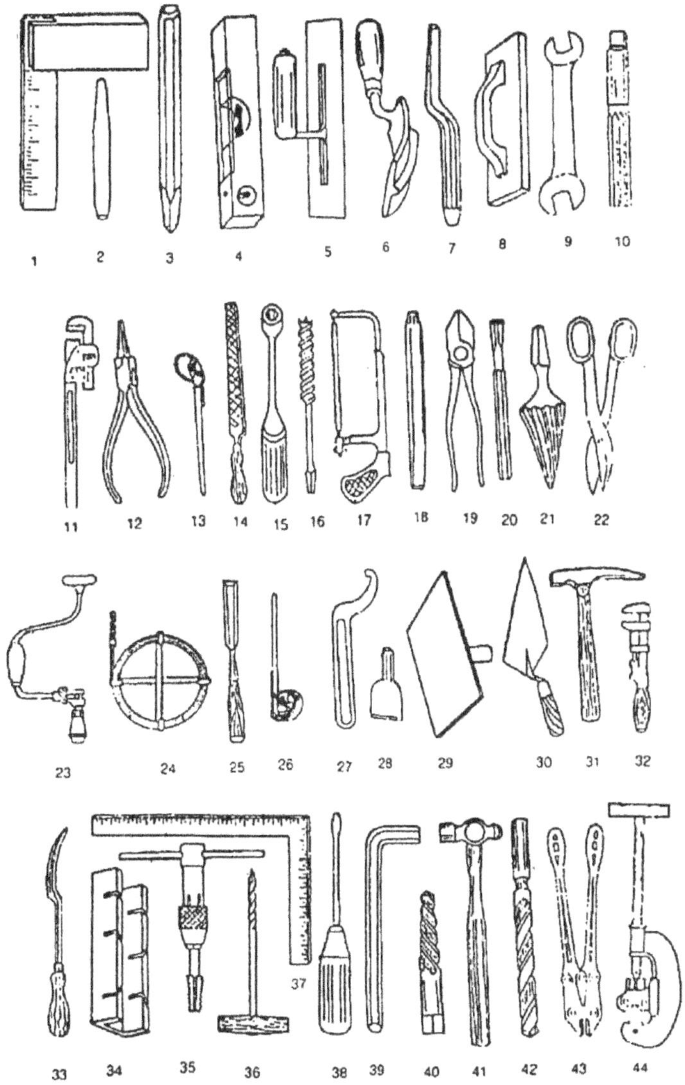

1. A "pipe reamer" is tool number 1.____
   A. 2 B. 10 C. 21 D. 24

2. A "mitre box" is tool number 2.____
   A. 1 B. 4 C. 25 D. 34

3. A "bolt cutter" is tool number 3.____
   A. 3 B. 25 C. 40 D. 43

4. The proper "drill bit" for wood is tool number 4.____
   A. 10 B. 16 C. 21 D. 40

5. A "ball peen" is tool number 5.____
   A. 20 B. 31 C. 33 D. 41

6. A "hawk" is tool number 6.____
   A. 5 B. 28 C. 29 D. 30

7. "Snips" is tool number 7.____
   A. 12 B. 19 C. 22 D. 43

8. A "bull point" is tool number 8.____
   A. 3 B. 7 C. 10 D. 20

9. An "open-end wrench" is tool number 9.____
   A. 9 B. 11 C. 15 D. 27

10. A "drift pin" is tool number 10.____
    A. 2 B. 3 C. 10 D. 40

11. A "pipe cutter" is tool number 11.____
    A. 17 B. 18 C. 28 D. 44

12. A "trowel" is tool number 12.____
    A. 6 B. 8 C. 28 D. 30

13. A "square" is tool number 13.____
    A. 4 B. 29 C. 34 D. 37

14. A "float" is tool number 14.____
    A. 8 B. 28 C. 29 D. 30

15. A "snake" is tool number 15.____
    A. 13 B. 24 C. 26 D. 36

KEY (CORRECT ANSWERS)

1.	C	6.	C	11.	D
2.	D	7.	C	12.	D
3.	D	8.	A	13.	D
4.	B	9.	A	14.	A
5.	D	10.	A	15.	B

TEST 2

DIRECTIONS: Each question or incomplete statement is followed by several suggested answers or completions. Select the one that BEST answers the question or completes the statement. *PRINT THE LETTER OF THE CORRECT ANSWER IN THE SPACE AT THE RIGHT.*

1. The tool shown at the right is a 1.____
   A. countersink
   B. counterbore
   C. star drill
   D. burring reamer

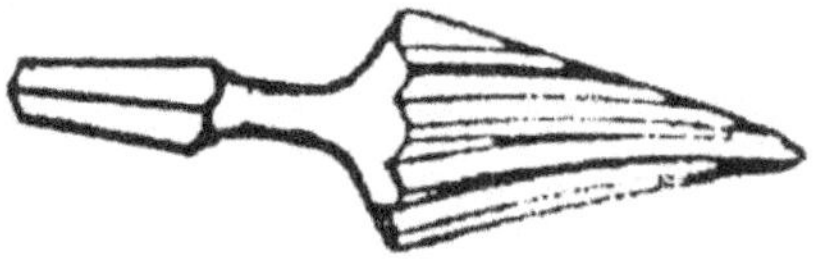

2. The saw shown at the right would be used to cut 2.____
   A. curved designs in thin wood
   B. strap iron
   C. asphalt tiles to fit against walls
   D. soft lead pipe

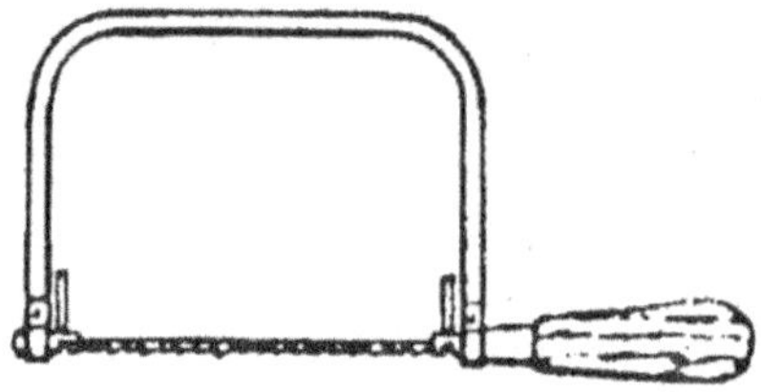

3. The tool shown at the right is a 3.____
   A. float
   B. finishing trowel
   C. hawk
   D. roofing seamer

4. The hammer shown to the right would be used by a 4.____
   A. carpenter
   B. bricklayer
   C. tinsmith
   D. plumber

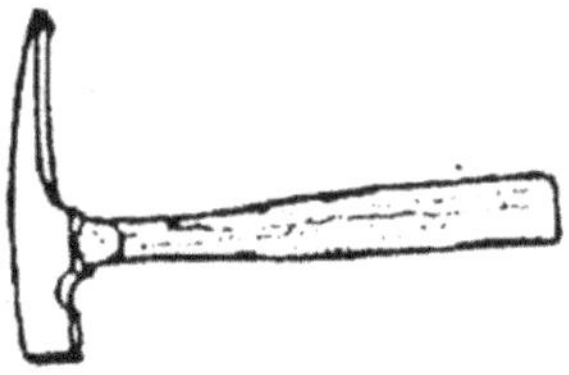

5. When drilling into a steel plate, the MOST likely cause for the breaking of a drill bit is 5.____
   A. too low a drill speed
   B. excessive cutting oil lubricant
   C. too much drill pressure
   D. using a bit with a dull point

6. Of the following, the MOST important advantage of a ratchet wrench over an open-end wrench is that the ratchet wrench 6.____
   A. can be used in a more limited space
   B. measures the torque applied
   C. will not strip the threads of a bolt
   D. is available for all sizes of hex bolts

7. The tool that holds the die when threading pipe is generally called a 7.____
   A. vise
   B. stock
   C. yoke
   D. coupling

8. A fitting used to join a small pipe at right angles to the middle of a large pie is called a 8.____
   A. union B. coupling C. cap D. reducing tee

9. Gaskets are commonly used between the flanges of large pipe joints to 9.____
   A. make a leakproof connection
   B. provide for expansion
   C. provide space for assembly
   D. adjust for poor alignment

10. The pipe fitting that should be used to connect a 1" pipe to a 1½" valve is called a 10.____
    A. reducing coupling
    B. nipple
    C. bushing
    D. union

11. The part of a drill press which is used to hold the drill bit is called a 11.____
    A. chuck B. collar C. bit D. vise

12. When grinding a flat chisel, it is GOOD practice to keep the chisel moving across the face of the grinding wheel in order to prevent 12.____
    A. grooving of the wheel
    B. burning of the chisel tip
    C. the wheel from vibrating
    D. the wheel from cracking

13. In order to determine if a surface is *truly* horizontal, it should be checked with a 13.____
    A. carpenters square
    B. plumb bob
    C. steel rule
    D. spirit level

14. A gauge of a nail indicates the 14.____
    A. length of the shank
    B. diameter of the head
    C. thickness of the head
    D. diameter of the shank

15. A tool can be used BOTH for scribing regular arcs and also for transferring dimensions is the 15.____
    A. trammel
    B. protractor
    C. scriber
    D. combination square

16. The devices for clamping sheet metal in place on a squaring shear are the 16.____
    A. clamps B. hold-downs C. guides D. square

17. When a hacksaw is used to cut out sheet metal, the BEST blade to use is one with ______ teeth per inch. 17.____
    A. 14 B. 18 C. 24 D. 32

18. A tool which may be attached to a drill press and used to cut circles of 2½" diameter or larger in sheet metal is the 18.____
    A. twist drill B. circular saw C. reamer D. hole saw

19. A versatile hand tool that can be used for a variety of sheet metalwork jobs such as bucking up rivet heads, straightening kinks in formed metal, forming seals, etc. is the 19.____
   A. hand dolly B. universal iron worker
   C. cupping tool D. set hammer

20. To make certain two points separated by a vertical distance of 8 feet are in perfect vertical alignment, it would be BEST to use a(n) 20.____
   A. surface gage B. height gage
   C. protractor D. plumb bob

21. A claw hammer is PROPERLY used for 21.____
   A. driving a cold chisel B. driving brads
   C. setting rivets D. flattening a ½" metal bar

22. It would NOT be good practice to tighten a 1" hexagon nut with a(n) _____ wrench. 22.____
   A. monkey B. 1" fixed open-end
   C. adjustable open-end D. stillson

23. Lock washers are used PRINCIPALLY with _____ screws. 23.____
   A. machine B. wood C. self-tapping D. lag

24. Toggle bolts are MOST appropriate for use to fasten conduit clamps to a 24.____
   A. steel column B. concrete wall
   C. hollow tile wall D. brick wall

25. If a 10-24 by ¾" machine screw is not available, the screw which could be MOST easily modified to use in an emergency is a 25.____
   A. 10-24 by ½" B. 12-24 by ¾"
   C. 10-2 by 1½" D. 8-24 by ¾"

26. Of the following tools, the one that should be used to cut thin-wall metal tubing is the 26.____
   A. reamer B. plier C. hacksaw D. broach

27. A wrench that can be used to tighten a nut to a specified tightness is a _____ wrench. 27.____
   A. bonney B. spud C. torque D. adjustable

28. The one of the following that will MOST likely show a "mushroomed" head is a 28.____
   A. cold chisel B. file cleaner
   C. screwdriver blade D. ratchet

29. A tool that is used to bend pipe is the 29.____
   A. lintel B. hickey C. collet D. brace

30. Before drilling a hole in a steel plate, an indentation should be made with a 30.____
A. center punch B. nail C. drill bit D. pin punch

KEY (CORRECT ANSWERS)

1.	D	11.	A	21.	B
2.	A	12.	A	22.	D
3.	A	13.	D	23.	A
4.	B	14.	D	24.	C
5.	C	15.	A	25.	C
6.	A	16.	B	26.	C
7.	B	17.	D	27.	C
8.	D	18.	D	28.	A
9.	A	19.	A	29.	B
10.	C	20.	D	30.	A

CLERICAL ABILITIES TEST

EXAMINATION SECTION

TEST 1

DIRECTIONS: Each question or incomplete statement is followed by several suggested answers or completions. Select the one that BEST answers the question or completes the statement. *PRINT THE LETTER OF THE CORRECT ANSWER IN THE SPACE AT THE RIGHT.*

Questions 1-10.

DIRECTIONS: Questions 1 through 10 consist of lines of names, dates, and numbers. For each question, you are to choose the option (A, B, C, or D) in Column II which EXACTLY matches the information in Column I. *PRINT THE LETTER OF THE CORRECT ANSWER IN THE SPACE AT THE RIGHT.*

SAMPLE QUESTION

<u>Column I</u>	<u>Column II</u>
Schneider 11/16/75 581932	A. Schneider 11/16/75 518932
	B. Schneider 11/16/75 581932
	C. Schnieder 11/16/75 581932
	D. Shnieder 11/16/75 518932

The correct answer is B. Only Option B shows the name, date, and number exactly as they are in Column I. Option A has a mistake in the number. Option C has a mistake in the name. Option D has a mistake in the name and in the number. Now answer Questions 1 through 10 in the same manner.

	<u>Column I</u>	<u>Column II</u>	
1.	Johnston 12/26/74 659251	A. Johnson 12/23/74 659251	1.____
		B. Johston 12/26/74 659251	
		C. Johnston 12/26/74 695251	
		D. Johnston 12/26/74 659251	
2.	Allison 1/26/75 9939256	A. Allison 1/26/75 9939256	2.____
		B. Alisson 1/26/75 9939256	
		C. Allison 1/26/76 9399256	
		D. Allison 1/26/75 9993356	
3.	Farrell 2/12/75 361251	A. Farell 2/21/75 361251	3.____
		B. Farrell 2/12/75 361251	
		C. Farrell 2/21/75 361251	
		D. Farrell 2/12/75 361151	

4. Guerrero 4/28/72 105689 — 4.____
A. Guererro 4/28/72 105689
B. Guererro 4/28/72 105986
C. Guerrero 4/28/72 105869
D. Guerrero 4/28/72 105689

5. McDonnell 6/05/73 478215 — 5.____
A. McDonnell 6/15/73 478215
B. McDonnell 6/05/73 478215
C. McDonnell 6/05/73 472815
D. MacDonell 6/05/73 478215

6. Shepard 3/31/71 075421 — 6.____
A. Sheperd 3/31/71 075421
B. Shepard 3/13/71 075421
C. Shepard 3/31/71 075421
D. Shepard 3/13/71 075241

7. Russell 4/01/69 031429 — 7.____
A. Russell 4/01/69 031429
B. Russell 4/10/69 034129
C. Russell 4/10/69 031429
D. Russell 4/01/69 034129

8. Phillips 10/16/68 961042 — 8.____
A. Philipps 10/16/68 961042
B. Phillips 10/16/68 960142
C. Phillips 10/16/68 961042
D. Philipps 10/16/68 916042

9. Campbell 11/21/72 624856 — 9.____
A. Campbell 11/21/72 624856
B. Campbell 11/21/72 624586
C. Campbell 11/21/72 624686
D. Campbel 11/21/72 624856

10. Patterson 9/18/71 76199176 — 10.____
A. Patterson 9/18/72 76191976
B. Patterson 9/18/71 76199176
C. Patterson 9/18/72 76199176
D. Patterson 9/18/71 76919176

Questions 11-15.

DIRECTIONS: Questions 11 through 15 consist of groups of numbers and letters which you are to compare. For each question, you are to choose the option (A, B,C, or D) in Column I which EXACTLY matches the group of numbers and letters given in Column I.

SAMPLE QUESTION

Column I	Column II
B92466	A. B92644
	B. B94266
	C. A92466
	D. B92466

The correct answer is D. Only Option D in Column II shows the group of numbers and letters EXACTLY as it appears in Column I. Now answer Questions 11 through 15 in the same manner.

	Column I	Column II	
11.	925AC5	A. 952CA5 B. 925AC5 C. 952AC5 D. 925CA6	11.____
12.	Y006925	A. Y060925 B. Y006295 C. Y006529 D. Y006925	12.____
13.	J236956	A. J236956 B. J326965 C. J239656 D. J932656	13.____
14.	AB6952	A. AB6952 B. AB9625 C. AB9652 D. AB6925	14.____
15.	X259361	A. X529361 B. X259631 C. X523961 D. X259361	15.____

Questions 16-25.

DIRECTIONS: Each of questions 16 through 25 consists of three lines of code letters and three lines of numbers. The numbers on each line should correspond with the code letters on the same line in accordance with the table below.

Code Letter	S	V	W	A	Q	M	X	E	G	K
Corresponding Number	0	1	2	3	4	5	5	7	8	9

On some of the lines, an error exists in the coding. Compare the letters and numbers in each question carefully. If you find an error or errors on:

only one of the lines in the question, mark your answer A;
any two lines in the question, mark your answer B;
all three lines in the question, mark your answer C;
none of the lines in the question, mark your answer D.

SAMPLE QUESTION

WQGKSXG	2489068
XEKVQMA	6591453
KMAESXV	9527061

In the above sample, the first line is correct since each code letter listed has the correct corresponding number. On the second line, an error exists because code letter E should have the number 7 instead of the number 5. On the third line, an error exists because the code letter A should have the number 3 instead of the number 2. Since there are errors in two of the three lines, the correct answer is B. Now answer Questions 16 through 25 in the same manner.

16. SWQEKGA 0247983
KEAVSXM 9731065
SSAXGKQ 0036894
16.____

17. QAMKMVS 4259510
MGGEASX 5897306
KSWMKWS 9125920
17.____

18. WKXQWVE 2964217
QKXXQVA 4966413
AWMXGVS 3253810
18.____

19. GMMKASE 8559307
AWVSKSW 3210902
QAVSVGK 4310189
19.____

20. XGKQSMK 6894049
QSVKEAS 4019730
GSMXKMV 8057951
20.____

21. AEKMWSG 3195208
MKQSVQK 5940149
XGQAEVW 6843712
21.____

22. XGMKAVS 6858310
SKMAWEQ 0953174
GVMEQSA 8167403
22.____

23. VQSKAVE 1489317
WQGKAEM 2489375
MEGKAWQ 5689324
23.____

24. XMQVSKG 6541098
QMEKEWS 4579720
KMEVGKG 9571983
24.____

25. GKVAMEW 88912572 25.____
AXMVKAE 3651937
KWAGMAV 9238531

Questions 26-35.

DIRECTIONS: Each of Questions 26 through 35 consists of a column of figures. For each question, add the column of figures and choose the correct answer from the four choices given.

26. 26.____
5,665.43
2,356.69
6,447.24
7,239.65

A. 20,698.01
B. 21,709.01
C. 21,718.01
D. 22,609.01

27. 27.____
817,209.55
264,354.29
82,368.76
849,964.89

A. 1,893.977.49
B. 1,989,988.39
C. 2,009,077.39
D. 2,013,897.49

28. 28.____
156,366.89
249,973.23
823,229.49
56,869.45

A. 1,286,439.06
B. 1,287,521.06
C. 1,297,539.06
D. 1,296,421.06

29. 29.____
23,422.15
149,696.24
238,377.53
86,289.79
505,533.63

A. 989,229.34
B. 999,879.34
C. 1,003,330.34
D. 1,023,329.34

30. 2,468,926.70
656,842.28
49,723.15
832,369.59 30.____

A. 3,218,062.72
B. 3,808,092.72
C. 4,007,861.72
D. 4,818,192.72

31. 524,201.52
7,775,678.51
8,345,299.63
40,628,898.08
31,374,670.07 31.____

A. 88,646,647.81
B. 88,646,747.91
C. 88,648,647.91
D. 88,648,747.81

32. 6,824,829.40
682,482.94
5,542,015.27
775,678.51
7,732,507.25 32.____

A. 21,557,513.37
B. 21,567,513.37
C. 22,567,503.37
D. 22,567,513.37

33. 22,109,405.58
6,097,093.43
5,050,073.99
8,118,050.05
4,313,980.82 33.____

A. 45,688,593.87
B. 45,688,603.87
C. 45,689,593.87
D. 45,689,603.87

34. 79,324,114.19
99,848,129.74
43,331,653.31
41,610,207.14 34.____

A. 264,114,104.38
B. 264,114,114.38
C. 265,114,114.38
D. 265,214,104.38

35. 33,729,653.94 35.____
5,959,342.58
26,052,715.47
4,452,669.52
7,079,953.59

A. 76,374,334.10
B. 76,375,334.10
C. 77,274,335.10
D. 77,275,335.10

Questions 36-40.

DIRECTIONS: Each of Questions 36 through 40 consists of a single number in Column I and four options in Column II. For each question, you are to choose the option (A, B, C, or D) in Column II which EXACTLY matches the number in Column I.

SAMPLE QUESTION

Column I	Column II
5965121	A. 5956121
	B. 5965121
	C. 5966121
	D. 5965211

The correct answer is B. Only Option B shows the number EXACTLY as it appears in Column I. Now answer Questions 36 through 40 in the same manner.

	Column I	Column II	
36.	9643242	A. 9643242	36.____
		B. 9462342	
		C. 9642442	
		D. 9463242	
37.	3572477	A. 3752477	37.____
		B. 3725477	
		C. 3572477	
		D. 3574277	
38.	5276101	A. 5267101	38.____
		B. 5726011	
		C. 5271601	
		D. 5276101	
39.	4469329	A. 4496329	39.____
		B. 4469329	
		C. 4496239	
		D. 4469239	

40. 2326308

A. 2236308
B. 2233608
C. 2326308
D. 2323608

40.____

KEY (CORRECT ANSWERS)

1.	D	11.	B	21.	A	31.	D
2.	A	12.	D	22.	C	32.	A
3.	B	13.	A	23.	B	33.	B
4.	D	14.	A	24.	D	34.	A
5.	B	15.	D	25.	A	35.	C
6.	C	16.	D	26.	B	36.	A
7.	A	17.	C	27.	D	37.	C
8.	C	18.	A	28.	A	38.	D
9.	A	19.	D	29.	C	39.	B
10.	B	20.	B	30.	C	40.	C

TEST 2

DIRECTIONS: Each question or incomplete statement is followed by several suggested answers or completions. Select the one that BEST answers the question or completes the statement. *PRINT THE LETTER OF THE CORRECT ANSWER IN THE SPACE AT THE RIGHT.*

Questions 1-5.

DIRECTIONS: Each of Questions 1 through 5 consists of a name and a dollar amount. In each question, the name and dollar amount in Column II should be an EXACT copy of the name and dollar amount in Column I. If there is:
a mistake only in the name, mark your answer A;
a mistake only in the dollar amount, mark your answer B;
a mistake in both the name and the dollar amount, mark your answer C;
no mistake in either the name or the dollar amount, mark your answer D.

SAMPLE QUESTION

Column I	Column II
George Peterson $125.50	George Petersson $125.50

Compare the name and dollar amount in Column II with the name and dollar amount in Column I. The name *Petersson* in Column II is spelled *Peterson* in Column I. The amount is the same in both columns. Since there is a mistake only in the name, the answer to the sample question is A. Now answer Questions 1 through 5 in the same manner.

	Column I	Column II	
1.	Susanne Shultz $3440	Susanne Schultz $3440	1.____
2.	Anibal P. Contrucci $2121.61	Anibel P. Contrucci $2112.61	2.____
3.	Eugenio Mendoza $12.45	Eugenio Mendozza $12.45	3.____
4.	Maurice Gluckstadt $4297	Maurice Gluckstadt $4297	4.____
5.	John Pampellonne $4656.94	John Pammpellonne $4566.94	5.____

Questions 6-11.

DIRECTIONS: Each of Questions 6 through 11 consist of a set of names and addresses, which you are to compare. In each question, the name and addresses in Column II should be an EXACT copy of the name and address in Column I. If there is:
- a mistake only in the name, mark your answer A;
- a mistake only in the address, mark your answer B;
- a mistake in both the name and address, mark your answer C;
- no mistake in either the name or address, mark your answer D.

SAMPLE QUESTION

Column I	Column II
Michael Filbert 456 Reade Street New York, N.Y. 10013	Michael Filbert 645 Reade Street New York, N.Y. 10013

Since there is a mistake only in the address (the street number should be 456 instead of 645), the answer to the sample question is B. Now answer Questions 6 through 11 in the same manner.

	Column I	Column II	
6.	Hilda Goettelmann 55 Lenox Rd. Brooklyn, N.Y. 11226	Hilda Goettelman 55 Lenox Ave. Brooklyn, N.Y. 11226	6.____
7.	Arthur Sherman 2522 Batchelder St. Brooklyn, N.Y. 11235	Arthur Sharman 2522 Batcheder St. Brooklyn, N.Y. 11253	7.____
8.	Ralph Barnett 300 West 28 Street New York, New York 10001	Ralph Barnett 300 West 28 Street New York, New York 10001	8.____
9.	George Goodwin 135 Palmer Avenue Staten Island, New York 10302	George Godwin 135 Palmer Avenue Staten Island, New York 10302	9.____
10.	Alonso Ramirez 232 West 79 Street New York, N.Y. 10024	Alonso Ramirez 223 West 79 Street New York, N.Y. 10024	10.____
11.	Cynthia Graham 149-34 83 Street Howard Beach, N.Y. 11414	Cynthia Graham 149-35 83 Street Howard Beach, N.Y. 11414	11.____

Questions 12-20.

DIRECTIONS: Questions 12 through 20 are problems in subtraction. For each question do the subtraction and select your answer from the four choices given.

12. 232,921.85
-179,587.68 12.____

A. 52,433.17
B. 52,434.17
C. 53,334.17
D. 53,343,17

13. 5,531,876.29
-3,897,158.36 13.____

A. 1,634,717.93
B. 1,644,718.93
C. 1,734,717.93
D. 1,7234,718.93

14. 1,482,658.22
-937,925.76 14.____

A. 544,633.46
B. 544,732.46
C. 545,632.46
D. 545,732.46

15. 937,828.17
-259,673.88 15.____

A. 678,154.29
B. 679,154.29
C. 688,155.39
D. 699,155.39

16. 760,412.38
-263,465.95 16.____

A. 496,046.43
B. 496,946.43
C. 496,956.43
D. 497,046.43

17. 3,203,902.26
-2,933,087.96 17.____

A. 260,814.30
B. 269,824.30
C. 270,814.30
D. 270,824.30

18. 1,023,468.71
-934,678.88 18.____

A. 88,780.83
B. 88,789.83
C. 88,880.83
D. 88,889.83

19. 831,549.47
-772,814.78 19.____

A. 58,734.69
B. 58,834.69
C. 59,735.69
D. 59,834.69

20. 6,306,181.74
-3,617,376.99 20.____

A. 2,687,904.99
B. 2,688,904.99
C. 2,689,804.99
D. 2,799,905.99

Questions 21-30.

DIRECTIONS: Each of Questions 21 through 30 consists of three lines of code letters and three lines of numbers. The numbers on each line should correspond with the code letters on the same line in accordance with the table below.

Code Letter	J	U	B	T	Y	D	K	R	L	P
Corresponding Number	0	1	2	3	4	5	5	7	8	9

On some of the lines, an error exists in the coding. Compare the letters and numbers in each question carefully. If you find an error or errors on:
only *one* of the lines in the question, mark your answer A;
any *two* lines in the question, mark your answer B;
all *three* lines in the question, mark your answer C;
none of the lines in the question, mark your answer D.

SAMPLE QUESTION

BJRPYUR 2079417
DTBPYKJ 5328460
YKLDBLT 4685283

In the above sample, the first line is correct since each code letter listed has the correct corresponding number. On the second line, an error exists because code letter P should have the number 9 instead of the number 8. The third line is correct since each code letter listed has the correct corresponding number. Since there is an error in *one* of the three lines, the correct answer is A. Now answer Questions 21 through 30 in the same manner.

21. BYPDTJL 2495308 21.____
PLRDTJU 9815301
DTJRYLK 5207486

22. RPBYRJK 7934706 22.____
PKTYLBU 9624821
KDLPJYR 6489047

23.	TPYBUJR	3942107	23.____
	BYRKPTU	2476931	
	DUKPYDL	5169458	
24.	KBYDLPL	6345898	24.____
	BLRKBRU	2876261	
	JTULDYB	0318542	
25.	LDPYDKR	8594567	25.____
	BDKDRJL	2565708	
	BDRPLUJ	2679810	
26.	PLRLBPU	9858291	26.____
	LPYKRDJ	88936750	
	TDKPDTR	3569527	
27.	RKURPBY	7617924	27.____
	RYUKPTJ	7426930	
	RTKPTJD	7369305	
28.	DYKPBJT	5469203	28.____
	KLPJBTL	6890238	
	TKPLBJP	3698209	
29.	BTPRJYL	2397148	29.____
	LDKUTYR	8561347	
	YDBLRPJ	4528190	
30.	ULPBKYT	1892643	30.____
	KPDTRBJ	6953720	
	YLKJPTB	4860932	

KEY (CORRECT ANSWERS)

1.	A	11.	D	21.	B
2.	C	12.	C	22.	C
3.	A	13.	A	23.	D
4.	D	14.	B	24.	B
5.	C	15.	A	25.	A
6.	C	16.	B	26.	C
7.	C	17.	C	27.	A
8.	D	18.	B	28.	D
9.	A	19.	A	29.	B
10.	B	20.	B	30.	D

FILING

EXAMINATION SECTION

TEST 1

Questions 1-9.

DIRECTIONS: An important part of the duties of an office worker in a public agency is to file office records. Questions 1 through 9 are designed to determine whether you can file records correctly. Each of these questions consists of four names. For each question, select the one of the four names that should be FOURTH if the four names were arranged in alphabetical order. *PRINT THE LETTER OF THE CORRECT ANSWER IN THE SPACE AT THE RIGHT.*

1. A. 6th National Bank
   B. Sexton Lock Co.
   C. The 69th Street League
   D. Thomas Saxon Corp.
   1.____

2. A. 4th Avenue Printing Co.
   B. The Four Corners Corp.
   C. Dr. Milton Fournet
   D. The Martin Fountaine Co.
   2.____

3. A. Mr. Chas. Le Mond
   B. Model Express, Inc.
   C. Lenox Enterprises
   D. Mobile Supply Co.
   3.____

4. A. Frank Waller Johnson
   B. Frank Walter Johnson
   C. Wilson Johnson
   D. Frank W. Johnson
   4.____

5. A. Miss Anne M. Carlsen
   B. Mrs. Albert S. Carlson
   C. Mr. Alan Ross Carlsen
   D. Dr. Anthony Ash Carlson
   5.____

6. A. Delaware Paper Co.
   B. William Del Ville
   C. Ralph A. Delmar
   D. Wm. K. Del Ville
   6.____

7. A. The Lloyd Disney Co.
   B. Mrs. Raymond Norris
   C. Oklahoma Envelope, Inc.
   D. Miss Esther O'Neill
   7.____

8. A. The Olympic Eraser Co.
   B. Mrs. Raymond Norris
   C. Oklahoma Envelope, Inc.
   D. Miss Esther O'Neill
   8.____

9. A. Patricia MacNamara
   B. Eleanor McNally
   C. Robt. MacPherson, Jr.
   D. Helen McNair
   9.____

Questions 10-21.

DIRECTIONS: Questions 10 through 21 are to be answered on the basis of the usual rules for alphabetical filing. For each question, indicate in the space at the right the letter preceding the name which should be THIRD in alphabetical order.

10. A. Russell Cohen B. Henry Cohn 10.____
C. Wesley Chambers D. Arthur Connors

11. A. Wanda Jenkins B. Pauline Jennings 11.____
C. Leslie Jantzenberg D. Rudy Jensen

12. A. Arnold Wilson B. Carlton Willson 12.____
C. Duncan Williamson D. Ezra Wilston

13. A. Joseph M. Buchman B. Gustave Bozzerman 13.____
C. Constantino Brunelli D. Armando Buccino

14. A. Barbara Waverly B. Corinne Warterdam 14.____
C. Dennis Waterman D. Harold Wartman

15. A. Jose Mejia B. Bernard Mendelsohn 15.____
C. Antonio Mejias D. Richard Mazzitelli

16. A. Hesselberg, Norman J. B. Hesselman, Nathan B. 16.____
C. Hazel, Robert S. D. Heintz, August J.

17. A. Oshins, Jerome B. Ohsie, Marjorie 17.____
C. O'Shaugn, F.J. D. O'Shea, Frances

18. A. Petrie, Joshua A. B. Pendleton, Oscar 18.____
C. Pertwee, Joshua D. Perkins, Warren G.

19. A. Morganstern, Alfred B. Morganstern, Albert 19.____
C. Monroe, Mildred D. Modesti, Ernest

20. A. More, Stewart B. Moorhead, Jay 20.____
C. Moore, Benjamin D. Moffat, Edith

21. A. Ramirez, Paul B. Revere, Pauline 21.____
C. Ramos, Felix D. Ramazotti, Angelo

KEY (CORRECT ANSWERS)

1. C
2. A
3. B
4. B
5. D

6. A
7. C
8. D
9. B
10. B

11. B
12. A
13. D
14. C
15. C

16. A
17. D
18. C
19. B
20. B

21. C

TEST 2

DIRECTIONS: Each question or incomplete statement is followed by several suggested answers or completions. Select the one that BEST answers the question or completes the statement. *PRINT THE LETTER OF THE CORRECT ANSWER IN THE SPACE AT THE RIGHT.*

Questions 1-4.

DIRECTIONS: Questions 1 through 4 are to be answered on the basis of the following alphabetical rules.

RULES FOR ALPHABETICAL FILING

Names of Individuals

The names of individuals are filed in strict alphabetical order, *first* according to the last name, *then* according to first name or initial, and *finally* according to middle name or initial. For example: George Allen precedes Edward Bell and Leonard Reston precedes Lucille Reston.

When last names are the same, for example, A. Green and Agnes Green, the one with the initial comes before the one with the name written out when the first initials are identical.

Prefixes such as De, O', Mac, Mc and Van are filed as written and are treated as part of the names to which they are connected. For example, Gladys McTeaque is filed before Frances Meadows.

1. If the following four names were put into an alphabetical list, what would the FIRST name on the list be? 1.____
   A. Wm. C. Paul
   B. W. Paul
   C. Alice Paul
   D. Alyce Paule

2. If the following four names were put into an alphabetical list, what would the THIRD name on the list be? 2.____
   A. I. MacCarthy
   B. Irene MacKarthy
   C. Ida McCaren
   D. I.A. McCarthy

3. If the following four names were put into an alphabetical list, what would the SECOND name on the list be? 3.____
   A. John Gilhooley
   B. Ramon Gonzalez
   C. Gerald Gilholy
   D. Samuel Gilvecchio

4. If the following four names were put into an alphabetical list, what would the FOURTH name on the list be? 4.____
   A. Michael Edwinn
   B. James Edwards
   C. Mary Edwin
   D. Carlo Edwards

Questions 5-9.

DIRECTIONS: Questions 5 through 9 consist of a group of names which are to be arranged in alphabetical order for filing.

5. Of the following, the name which should be filed FIRST is 5.____
   A. Joseph J. Meadeen B. Gerard L. Meader
   C. John F. Madcar D. Philip F. Malder

6. Of the following, the name which should be filed LAST is 6.____
   A. Stephen Fischer B. Benjamin Fitchmann
   C. Thomas Fishman D. Augustus S. Fisher

7. The name which should be filed SECOND is 7.____
   A. Yeatman, Frances B. Yeaton, C.S.
   C. Yeatman, R.M. D. Yeats, John

8. The name which should be filed THIRD is 8.____
   A. Hauser, Ann B. Hauptmann, Jane
   C. Hauster, Mary D. Rauprich, Julia

9. The name which should be filed SECOND is 9.____
   A. Flora McDougall B. Fred E. MacDowell
   C. Juanita Mendez D. James A. Madden

Questions 10-14.

DIRECTIONS: Questions 10 through 14 are to be answered based on an alphabetical arrangement of the following list of names.

Walker, Carol J.	Wacht, Michael	Wade, Ethel
Wall, Fredrick	Wall, Francis	Wall, Frank
Wachs, Paul	Walker, Carol L.	Wagner, Arthur
Walters, Daniel	Wade, Ellen	Wald, William
Wagner, Allen	Walters, David	Walker, Carmen

10. The 4th name on the alphabetized list would be 10.____
   A. Wade, Ellen B. Wade, Ethel
   C. Wagner, Allen D. Wagner, Arthur

11. The 7th name on the alphabetized list would be 11.____
   A. Walker, Carmen B. Walker, Carol J.
   C. Walker, Carol L. D. Wald, William

12. The name that would come immediately AFTER Wagner, Arthur on the alphabetized list would be 12.____
   A. Wade, Ethel B. Wagner, Allen
   C. Wald, William D. Walker, Carol L.

13. The name that would come immediately BEFORE Wall, Frank would be 13.____
    A. Wall, Francis B. Wall, Fredrick
    C. Walters, David D. Walters, Daniel

14. The 12th name on the alphabetized list would be 14.____
    A. Walker, Carol L. B. Wald, William
    C. Wall, Francis D. Wall, Frank

KEY (CORRECT ANSWERS)

1.	C	6.	B	11.	D
2.	C	7.	C	12.	C
3.	A	8.	A	13.	A
4.	A	9.	D	14.	D
5.	C	10.	B		

TEST 3

DIRECTIONS: Each question or incomplete statement is followed by several suggested answers or completions. Select the one that BEST answers the question or completes the statement. *PRINT THE LETTER OF THE CORRECT ANSWER IN THE SPACE AT THE RIGHT.*

Questions 1-8.

DIRECTIONS: Questions 1 through 8 are based on the Rules of Alphabetical Filing given below. Read these rules carefully before answering the questions.

Names of People

1. The names of people are filed in strict alphabetical order, first according to the last name, then according to first name or initial, and finally according to middle name or initial. For example: George Allen comes before Edward Bell, and Leonard P. Reston comes before Lucille B. Reston.

2. When last names are the same, for example, A. Green and Agnes Green, the one with the initial comes before the one with the name written out when the first initials are identical.

3. When first and last names are alike and the middle name is given, for example, John David Doe and John Devoe Doe, the names should be filed in alphabetical order of the middle names.

4. When first and last names are the same, a name without a middle initial comes before one with a middle name or initial. For example, John Doe comes before John A. Doe and John Alan Doe.

5. When first and last names are the same, a name with a middle initial comes before one with a middle name beginning with the same initial. For example, Jack R. Hertz comes before Jack Richard Hertz.

6. Prefixes such as De, O', Mac, Mc, and Van are filed as written and are treated as part of the names to which they are connected. For example, Robert O'Dea is filed before David Olsen.

7. Abbreviated names are treated as if they were spelled out. For example: Chas. is filed as Charles and Thos. is filed as Thomas.

8. Titles and designations such as Dr., Mr., and Prof. are disregarded in filing.

Names of Organizations

1. The names of business organizations are filed according to the order in which each word in the name appears. When an organization name bears the name of a person, it is filed according to the rules for filing names of people as given above. For example: William Smith Service Co. comes before Television Distributors, Inc.

2. Where bureau, board, office or department appears as the first part of the title of a governmental agency, that agency should be filed under the word in the title expressing the chief function of the agency. For example, Bureau of Budget would be filed as if written Budget, (Bureau of the). The Department of Personnel would be filed as if written Personnel, (Department of).

3. When the following words are part of an organization, they are disregarded: the, of, and.

4. When there are numbers in a name, they are treated as if they were spelled out. For example: 10th Street Bootery is filed as Tenth Street Bootery.

Each question from 1 through 8 contains four names numbered from 1 through 4 but not necessarily numbered in correct filing order. Answer each question by choosing the letter corresponding to the CORRECT filing order of the four names in accordance with the above rules.

SAMPLE QUESTION:
I. Robert J. Smith
II. R. Jeffrey Smith
III. Dr. A. Smythe
IV. Allen R. Smithers

A. I, II, III, IV B. III, I, II, IV C. II, I, IV, III D. III, II, I, IV

Since the correct filing order, in accordance with the above rules is II I, IV, III, the correct answer Is C.

1. I. J. Chester VanClief II. John C. Van Clief 1.____
III. J. VanCleve IV. Mary L. Vance

The CORRECT answer is:
A. IV, III, I, II B. IV, III, II, I C. III, I, II, IV D. III, IV, I, II

2. I. Community Development Agency II. Department of Social Services 2.____
III. Board of Estimate IV. Bureau of Gas and Electricity

The CORRECT answer is:
A. III, IV, I, II B. 1, II, IV, III C. II, I, III, IV D. I, III, IV, II

3. I. Dr. Chas. K. Dahlman II. F. & A. Delivery Service 3.____
III. Department of Water Supply IV. Demano Men's Custom Tailors

The CORRECT answer is:
A. I, II, III, IV B. I, IV, II, III C. IV, I, II, III D. IV, I, III, II

4. I. 48th Street Theater II. Fourteenth Street Day Care Center 4.____
III. Professor A. Cartwright IV. Albert F. McCarthy

The CORRECT answer is:
A. IV, II, I, III B. IV, III, I, II C. III, II, I, IV D. III, I, II, IV

5. I. Frances D'Arcy II. Mario L. DelAmato 5.____
III. William R. Diamond IV. Robert J. DuBarry

The CORRECT answer is:
A. I, II, IV, III B. II, I, III, IV C. I, II, III, IV D. II, I, III, IV

6. I. Evelyn H. D'Amelio II. Jane R. Bailey 6.____
III. Robert Bailey IV. Frank Baily

The CORRECT answer is:
A. I, II, III, IV B. I, III, II, IV C. II, III, IV, I D. III, II, IV, I

7. I. Department of Markets 7.____
II. Bureau of Handicapped Children
III. Housing Authority Administration Building
IV. Board of Pharmacy

The CORRECT answer is:
A. II, I, III, IV B. I, II, IV, III C. I, II, III, IV D. III, II, I, IV

8. I. William A. Shea Stadium II. Rapid Speed Taxi Co. 8.____
III. Harry Stampler's Rotisserie III. Wilhelm Albert Shea

The CORRECT answer is:
A. II, III, IV, I B. IV, I, III, II C. II, IV, I, III D. III, IV, I, II

Questions 9-18.

DIRECTIONS: Questions 9 through 18 each show in Column I names written on four ledger cards (lettered w, x, y, z) which have to be filed. You are to choose the option (lettered A, B, C, or D) in Column II which BEST represents the proper order for filing the cards.

SAMPLE

COLUMN I	COLUMN II
w. John Stevens	A. w, y, z, x
x. John D. Stevenson	B. y, w, z, x
y. Joan Stevens	C. x, y, w, z
z. J. Stevenson	D. x, w, y, z

The correct way to file the cards is:
y. Joan Stevens
w. John Stevens
z. J. Stevenson
x. John D. Stevenson

The correct order is shown by the letters y, w, z, x in that sequence. Since, in Column II, B appears in front of the letters y, w, z, x in that sequence, B is the correct answer to the sample question.

Now answer the following questions, using the same procedure.

9. COLUMN I | COLUMN II | 9.____
w. Juan Montoya | A. y, z, x, w
x. Manuel Montenegro | B. z, y, x, w
y. Victor Matos | C. z, y, w, x
z. Victoria Maltos | D. y, x, z, w

10. COLUMN I | COLUMN II | 10.____
w. Frank Carlson | A. z, x, w, y
x. Robert Carlson | B. z, y, x, w
y. George Carlson | C. w, y, z, x
z. Frank Carlton | D. w, z, y, x

11. COLUMN I | COLUMN II | 11.____
w. Carmine Rivera | A. y, w, x, z
x. Jose Rivera | B. y, x, w, z
y. Frank River | C. w, x, y, z
z. Joan Rivers | D. w, x, z, y

12. COLUMN I | COLUMN II | 12.____
w. Jerome Mathews | A. w, y, z, x
x. Scott A. Matthew | B. z, y, x, w
y. Charles B. Matthew | C. z, w, x, y
z. Scott C. Mathewsw | D. w, z, y, x

13. COLUMN I | COLUMN II | 13.____
w. John McMahan | A. w, x, y, z
x. John P. MacMahan | B. y, x, z, w
y. Joseph DeMayo | C. x, w, y, z
z. Joseph D. Mayo | D. y, x, w, z

14. COLUMN I | COLUMN II | 14.____
w. Raymond Martinez | A. z, x, y, w
x. Ramon Martinez | B. z, y, x, w
y. Prof. Ray Martinez | C. z, w, y, x
z. Dr. Raymond Martin | D. y, x, w, z

15. COLUMN I | COLUMN II | 15.____

	COLUMN I	COLUMN II
w.	Mr. Robert Vincent Mackintosh	A. y, x, z, w
x.	Robert Reginald Macintosh	B. x, w, z, y
y.	Roger V. McIntosh	C. x, w, y, z
z.	Robert R. Mackintosh	D. x, z, w, y

16. 16.____

	COLUMN I	COLUMN II
w.	Dr. D. V. Facsone	A. y, w, z, x
x.	Prof. David Fascone	B. w, y, x, z
y.	Donald Facsone	C. w, y, z, x
z.	Mrs. D. Fascone	D. z, w, x, y

17. 17.____

	COLUMN I	COLUMN II
w.	Johnathan Q. Addams	A. z, x, w, y
x.	John Quincy Adams	B. z, x, y, w
y.	J. Quincy Addams	C. y, w, x, z
z.	Jerimiah Adams	D. x, w, z, y

18. 18.____

	COLUMN I	COLUMN II
w.	Nehimiah Persoff	A. w, z, x, y
x.	Newton Pershing	B. x, z, y, w
y.	Newman Perring	C. y, x, w, z
z.	Nelson Persons	D. z, y, w, x

KEY (CORRECT ANSWERS)

1.	A	6.	D	11.	A	16.	C
2.	D	7.	D	12.	D	17.	B
3.	B	8.	C	13.	B	18.	C
4.	D	9.	B	14.	A		
5.	C	10.	C	15.	D		

TEST 4

Questions 1-13.

DIRECTIONS: Each question from 1 through 13 contains four names. For each question, choose the name that should be FIRST if he four names are to be arranged in alphabetical order in accordance with the Rule for Alphabetical Filing of Names of People given below. Read this rule carefully. Then, for each question, mark your answer space with the letter that is next to the name that should be first in alphabetical order.

RULE FOR ALPHABETICAL FILING OF NAMES OF PEOPLE

The names of people are filed in strict alphabetical order, first according to the last name, then according to the first name. For example; George Allen comes before Edward Bell, and Alice Reston comes before Lucille Reston.

SAMPLE QUESTION
A. Roger Smith (2)
B. Joan Smythe (4)
C. Alan Smith (1)
D. James Smithe (3)

The number in parentheses show the proper alphabetical order in which these names should be filed. Since the name that should be filed FIRST is Alan Smith, the correct answer to the sample question is C.

1. A. William Claremont B. Antonio Clements 1.____
C. Anthony Clemente D. William Claymont

2. A. Wayne Fumando B. Sarah Femando 2.____
C. Susan Fumando D. Wilson Femando

3. A. Wilbur Hanson B. Wm. Hansen 3.____
C. Robert Hansen D. Thomas Hanson

4. A. George St. John B. Thomas Santos 4.____
C. Frances Starks D. Mary S. Stranum

5. A. Franklin Carrol B. Timothy Carrol 5.____
C. Timothy S. Carol D. Frank F. Carroll

6. A. Christie-Barry Storage B. John Christie-Barry 6.____
C. The Christie-Barry Company D. Anne Christie-Barrie

7. A. Inter State Travel Co. A. Interstate Car Rental 7.____
C. Inter State Trucking D. Interstate Lending Inst.

8. A. The Los Angeles Tile Co. 8.____
   B. Anita F. Los
   C. The Lost & Found Detective Agency
   D. Jason Los-Brio

9. A. Prince Charles B. Prince Charles Coiffures 9.____
   C. Chas. F. Prince D. Thomas A. Charles

10. A. U.S. Dept. of Agriculture B. United States Aircraft Co. 10.____
    C. U.S. Air Transport, Inc. D. The United Union

11. A. Meyer's Art Shop B. Frank B. Meyer 11.____
    C. Meyers' Paint Store D. Meyer and Goldberg

12. A. David Des Laurier B. Des Moines Flower Shop 12.____
    C. Henry Desanto D. Mary L. Desta

13. A. Jeffrey Van Der Meer B. Jeffrey M. Vander 13.____
    C. Jeffrey Van D. Wallace Meer

KEY (CORRECT ANSWERS)

1.	A	6.	D	11.	A
2.	B	7.	B	12.	C
3.	C	8.	B	13.	D
4.	A	9.	D		
5.	C	10.	C		

TEST 5

Questions 1-10.

DIRECTIONS: Questions 1 through 10 are to be answered on the basis of the usual rules of filing. Column I lists, next to the numbers 1 to 10, the names of 10 clinic patients. Column II lists, next to the letters A to D, the headings of file drawers into which you are to place the records of these patients. For each question, indicate in the space at the right the letter preceding the heading of the file drawer in which the record should be filed.

	COLUMN I	COLUMN II	
1.	Charles Coughlin	A. Cab-Cep	1.____
2.	Mary Carstairs	B. Ceq-Cho	2.____
3.	Joseph Collin	C. Chr-Coj	3.____
4.	Thomas Chelsey	D. Cok-Czy	4.____
5.	Cedric Chalmers		5.____
6.	Mae Clarke		6.____
7.	Dora Copperhead		7.____
8.	Arnold Cohn		8.____
9.	Charlotte Crumboldt		9.____
10.	Frances Celine		10.____

Questions 11-18.

DIRECTIONS: Questions 11 to 18 are to be answered on the basis of the usual rules of filing. Column I lists, next to the numbers 11 to 18, the names of 8 clinic patients. Column II lists, next to the letters A to O, the headings of file drawers into which you are to place the records of these patients. For each question, indicate in the space at the right the letter preceding the heading of the file drawer in which the record should be filed.

COLUMN I	COLUMN II	
11. Thomas Adams	A. Aab-Abi	11.____
	B. Abj-Ach	
12. Joseph Albert	C. Aci-Aco	12.____
	D. Acp-Ada	
13. Frank Anaster	E. Adb-Afr	13.____
	F. Afs-Ago	
14. Charles Abt	G. Agp-Ahz	14.____
	H. Aia-Ako	
15. John Alfred	I. Akp-Ald	15.____
	J. Ale-Amo	
16. Louis Aron	K. Amp-Aor	16.____
	L. Aos-Apr	
17. Francis Amos	M. Aps-Asi	17.____
	N. Asj-Ati	
18. William Adler	O. Atj-Awz	18.____

Questions 19-28.

DIRECTIONS: Questions 19 through 28 are to be answered on the basis of the usual rules of filing. Column I lists, next to the numbers 19 through 28, the names of 10 clinic patients. Column II lists, next to the letters A to D the headings of file drawers into which you are to place the medical records of these patients. For each question, indicate in the space at the right the letter preceding the heading of the file drawer in which the record should be filed.

COLUMN I	COLUMN II	
19. Frank Shea	A. Sab-Sej	19.____
20. Rose Seaborn	B. Sek-Sio	20.____
21. Samuel Smollin	C. Sip-Soo	21.____
22. Thomas Shur	D. Sop-Syz	22.____
23. Ben Schaefer		23.____
24. Shirley Strauss		24.____
25. Harry Spiro		25.____
26. Dora Skelly		26.____
27. Sylvia Smith		27.____
28. Arnold Selz		28.____

KEY (CORRECT ANSWERS)

1.	D	11.	D	21.	C
2.	A	12.	I	22.	B
3.	D	13.	K	23.	A
4.	B	14.	B	24.	D
5.	B	15.	J	25.	D
6.	C	16.	M	26.	C
7.	D	17.	J	27.	C
8.	C	18.	E	28.	B
9.	D	19.	B		
10.	A	20.	A		

CODING

COMMENTARY

An ingenious question-type called coding, involving elements of alphabetizing, filing, name and number comparison, and evaluative judgment and application, has currently won wide acceptance in testing circles for measuring clerical aptitude and general ability, particularly on the senior (middle) grades (levels).

While the directions for this question-type usually vary in detail, the candidate is generally asked to consider groups of names, codes, and numbers, and, then, according to a given plan, to arrange codes in alphabetic order; to arrange these in numerical sequence; to re-arrange columns of names and numbers in correct order; to espy errors in coding; to choose the correct coding arrangement in consonance with the given directions and examples, etc.

This question-type appears to have few parameters in respect to form, substance, or degree of difficulty.

Accordingly, acquaintance with, and practice in the coding question is recommended for the serious candidate.

EXAMINATION SECTION
TEST 1

DIRECTIONS: Questions 1 through 10 are to be answered on the basis of the following Code Table. In this table every letter has a corresponding code number to be punched. Each question contains three lines of letters and code numbers. In each line, the code numbers should correspond with the letters in accordance with the table.

Letter	M	X	R	T	W	A	E	Q	Z	C
Code	1	2	3	4	5	6	7	8	9	0

On some of the lines, an error exists in the coding. Compare the letters and numbers in each question carefully. If you find an error or errors on

only *one* of the lines in the question, mark your answer A;
any *two* lines in the question, mark your answer B;
all *three* lines in the question, mark your answer C;
none of the lines in the question, mark your answer D.

SAMPLE QUESTION

XAQMZMRQ - 26819138
RAERQEX - 3573872
TMZCMTZA - 46901496

In the above sample, the first line is correct since each letter, as listed, has the correct corresponding code number.
In the second line, an error exists because the letter A should have the code number 6 instead of 5.
In the third line, an error exists because the letter W should have the code number 5 instead of 6.
Since there are errors in two of the three lines, your answer should be B.

1. EQRMATTR - 78316443   1.____
   MACWXRQW - 16052385
   XZEMCAR - 2971063

2. CZEMRXQ - 0971238   2.____
   XMTARET - 2146374
   WCEARWEC - 50863570

3. CEXAWRQZ - 07265389   3.____
   RCRMMZQT - 33011984
   ACMZWTEX - 60195472

4. XRCZQZWR - 23089953   4.____
   CMRQCAET - 01389574
   ZXRWTECM - 92345701

5.	AXMTRAWR	-	62134653	5.____
	EQQCZCEW	-	77809075	
	MAZQARTM	-	16086341	
6.	WRWQCTRM	-	53580431	6.____
	CXMWAERZ	-	02156739	
	RCQEWWME	-	30865517	
7.	CRMECEAX	-	03170762	7.____
	MZCTRXRQ	-	19043238	
	XXZREMEW	-	22937175	
8.	MRCXQEAX	-	13928762	8.____
	WAMZTRMZ	-	65194319	
	ECXARWXC	-	70263520	
9.	MAWXECRQ	-	16527038	9.____
	RXQEAETM	-	32876741	
	RXEWMCZQ	-	32751098	
10.	MRQZCATE	-	13890647	10.____
	WCETRXAW	-	50743625	
	CZWMCERT	-	09510734	

KEY (CORRECT ANSWERS)

1. D
2. B
3. A
4. C
5. C
6. A
7. D
8. B
9. D
10. A

TEST 2

DIRECTIONS: Questions 1 through 6 consist of three lines of code letters and numbers. The numbers on each, line should correspond with the code letters on the same line in accordance with the table below.

Code Letter	F	X	L	M	R	W	T	S	B	H
Corresponding Number	0	1	2	3	4	5	6	7	8	9

On some of the lines, an error exists in the coding. Compare the letters and numbers in each question carefully. If you find an error or errors on

only *one* of the lines in the question, mark your answer A;
any *two* lines in the question, mark your answer B;
all *three* lines in the question, mark your answer C;
none of the lines in the question, mark your answer D.

SAMPLE QUESTION

LTSXHMF 2671930
TBRWHLM 6845913
SXLBFMR 5128034

In the above sample, the first line is correct since each code letter listed has the correct corresponding number.

On the second line, an error exists because code letter L should have the number 2 instead of the number 1.

On the third line, an error exists because the code letter S should have the number 7 instead of the number 5.

Since there are errors on two of the three lines, the correct answer is B.

1. XMWBHLR 1358924 1.____
FWSLRHX 0572491
MTXBLTS 3618267

2. XTLSMRF 1627340 2.____
BMHRFLT 8394026
HLTSWRX 9267451

3. LMBSFXS 2387016 3.____
RWLMBSX 4532871
SMFXBHW 7301894

4. RSTWTSML 47657632 4.____
LXRMHFBS 21439087
FTLBMRWX 06273451

5. XSRSBWFM 17478603 5.____
BRMXRMXT 84314216
XSTFBWRL 17609542

6. TMSBXHLS 63781927 6.____
RBSFLFWM 48702053
MHFXWTRS 39015647

KEY (CORRECT ANSWERS)

1. D
2. A
3. C
4. B
5. C
6. D

TEST 3

DIRECTIONS: Questions 1 through 5 consist of three lines of code letters and numbers. The numbers on each line should correspond with the code letters on the same line in accordance with the table below.

Code Letter	P	L	I	J	B	O	H	U	C	G
Corresponding Number	0	1	2	3	4	5	6	7	8	9

On some of the lines, an error exists in the coding. Compare the letters and numbers in each question carefully. If you find an error or errors on

only *one* of the lines in the question, mark your answer A;
any *two* lines in the question, mark your answer B;
all *three* lines in the question, mark your answer C;
none of the lines in the question, mark your answer D.

SAMPLE QUESTION

JHOILCP 3652180
BICLGUP 4286970
UCIBHLJ 5824613

In the above sample, the first line is correct since each code letter listed has the correct corresponding number.
On the second line, an error exists because code letter L should have the number 1 instead of the number 6.
On the third line an error exists because the code letter U should have the number 7 instead of the number 5.
Since there are errors on two of the three lines, the correct answer is B.

1. BULJCIP 4713920 — 1. ____
HIGPOUL 6290571
OCUHJBI 5876342

2. CUBLOIJ 8741023 — 2. ____
LCLGCLB 1818914
JPUHIOC 3076158

3. OIJGCBPO 52398405 — 3. ____
UHPBLIOP 76041250
CLUIPGPC 81720908

4. BPCOUOJI 40875732 — 4. ____
UOHCIPLB 75682014
GLHUUCBJ 92677843

5. HOIOHJLH 65256361 — 5. ____
IOJJHHBP 25536640
OJHBJOPI 53642502

KEY (CORRECT ANSWERS)

1. A
2. C
3. D
4. B
5. C

TEST 4

DIRECTIONS: Questions 1 through 5 consist of three lines of code letters and numbers. The numbers on each line should correspond with the code letters on the same line in accordance with the table below.

Code Letters	Q	S	L	Y	M	0	U	N	W	Z
Corresponding Numbers	1	2	3	4	5	6	7	8	9	0

On some of the lines, an error exists in the coding. Compare the letters and numbers in each question carefully. If you find an error on

only *one* of the lines in the question, mark your answer A;
any *two* lines in the question, mark your answer B;
all *three* lines in the question, mark your answer C;
none of the lines in the question, mark your answer D.

SAMPLE QUESTION

MOQNWZQS 56189012
QWNMOLYU 19865347
LONLMYWN 36835489

In the above sample, the first line is correct since each code letter, as listed, has the correct corresponding number.
On the second line, an error exists because code letter M should have the number 5 instead of the number 6.
On the third line an error exists because the code letter W should have the number 9 instead of the number 8.
Since there are errors on two of the three lines, the correct answer is B.

1. SMUWOLQN 25796318 1.____
ULSQNMZL 73218503
NMYQZUSL 85410723

2. YUWWMYQZ 47995410 2.____
SOSOSQSO 26262126
ZUNLWMYW 07839549

3. QULSWZYN 17329045 3.____
ZYLQWOYF 04319639
QLUYWZSO 13749026

4. NLQZOYUM 83106475 4.____
SQMUWZOM 21579065
MMYWMZSQ 55498021

5. NQLOWZZU 81319007 5.____
SMYLUNZO 25347806
UWMSNZOL 79528013

KEY (CORRECT ANSWERS)

1. D
2. D
3. B
4. A
5. C

TEST 5

DIRECTIONS: Answer Questions 1 through 6 *SOLELY* on the basis of the chart and the instructions given below.

Toll Rate	$.25	$.30	$.45	$.60	$.75	$8.90	$1.20	$2.50
Classification Number of Vehicle	1	2	3	4	5	6	7	8

Assume that each of the amounts of money on the above chart is a toll rate charged for a type of vehicle and that the number immediately below each amount is the classification number for that type of vehicle. For instance, "1" is the classification number for a vehicle paying a $.25 toll; "2" is the classification number for a vehicle paying a $.30 toll; and so forth.
In each question, a series of tolls is given in Column I. Column II gives four different arrangements of classification numbers. You are to pick the answer (A, B, C, or D) in Column II that gives the classification numbers that match the tolls in Column I and are in the same order as the tolls in Column I.

SAMPLE QUESTION

Column I	Column II
$.30, $.90, $2.50, $.45	A. 2, 6, 8, 2
	B. 2, 8, 6, 3
	C. 2, 6, 8, 3
	D. 1, 6, 8, 3

According to the chart, the classification numbers that correspond to these toll rates are as follows: $.30 - 2, $.90 - 6, $2.50 - 8, $.45 -3. Therefore, the right answer is 2, 6, 8, 3. The answer is C in Column II.
Do the following questions in the same way.

Column I	Column II	
1. $.60, $.30, $.90, $1.20, $.60	A. 4, 6, 2, 8, 4	1.____
	B. 4, 2, 6, 7, 4	
	C. 2, 4, 7, 6, 2	
	D. 2, 4, 6, 7, 4	
2. $.90, $.45, $.25, $.45, $2.50, $.75	A. 6, 3, 1, 3, 8, 3	2.____
	B. 6, 3, 3, 1, 8, 5	
	C. 6, 1, 3, 3, 8, 5	
	D. 6, 3, 1, 3, 8, 5	
3. $.45, $.75, $1.20, $.25, $.25, $.30, $.45	A. 3, 5, 7, 1, 1, 2, 3	3.____
	B. 5, 3, 7, 1, 1, 2, 3	
	C. 3, 5, 7, 1, 2, 1, 3	
	D. 3, 7, 5, 1, 1, 2, 3	
4. $1.20, $2.50, $.45, $.90, $1.20, $.75, $.25	A. 7, 8, 5, 6, 7, 5, 1	4.____
	B. 7, 8, 3, 7, 6, 5, 1	
	C. 7, 8, 3, 6, 7, 5, 1	
	D. 7, 8, 3, 6, 7, 1, 5	

5. $2.50, $1.20, $.90, $.25, $.60, $.45, $.30

A. 8, 6, 7, 1, 4, 3, 2
B. 8, 7, 5, 1, 4, 3, 2
C. 8, 7, 6, 2, 4, 3, 2
D. 8, 7, 6, 1, 4, 3, 2

5.____

6. $.75, $.25, $.45, $.60, $.90, $.30, $2.50

A. 5, 1, 3, 2, 4, 6, 8
B. 5, 1, 3, 4, 2, 6, 8
C. 5, 1, 3, 4, 6, 2, 8
D. 5, 3, 1, 4, 6, 2, 8

6.____

KEY (CORRECT ANSWERS)

1. B
2. D
3. A
4. C
5. D
6. C

TEST 6

DIRECTIONS: Answer Questions 1 through 10 on the basis of the following information:
A code number for any item is obtained by combining the date of delivery, number of units received, and number of units used. The first two digits represent the day of the month, the third and fourth digits represent the month, and the fifth and sixth digits represent the year.
The number following the letter R represents the number of units received and the number following the letter U represents the number of units used.
For example, the code number 120603-R5690-U1001 indicates that a delivery of 5,690 units was made on June 12, 2003 of which 1,001 units were used.

Questions 1-6.

DIRECTIONS: Using the chart below, answer Questions 1 through 6 by choosing the letter (A, B, C, or D) in which the supplier and stock number correspond to the code number given.

Supplier	Stock Number	Number of Units Received	Delivery Date	Number of Units Used
Stony	38390	8300	May 11, 2002	3800
Stoney	39803	1780	September 15, 2003	1703
Nievo	21220	5527	October 10, 2003	5007
Nieve	38903	1733	August 5, 2003	1703
Monte	39213	5527	October 10, 2002	5007
Stony	38890	3308	December 9, 2002	3300
Stony	83930	3880	September 12, 2002	380
Nevo	47101	485	June 11, 2002	231
Nievo	12122	5725	May 11, 2003	5201
Neve	47101	9721	August 15, 2003	8207
Nievo	21120	2275	January 7, 2002	2175
Rosa	41210	3821	March 3, 2003	2710
Stony	38890	3308	September 12, 2002	3300
Dinal	54921	1711	April 2, 2003	1117
Stony	33890	8038	March 5, 2003	3300
Dinal	54721	1171	March 2, 2002	717
Claridge	81927	3308	April 5, 2003	3088
Nievo	21122	4878	June 7, 2002	3492
Haley	39670	8300	December 23, 2003	5300

1. Code No. 120902-R3308-U3300 1.____

   A. Nievo - 12122
   B. Stony - 83930
   C. Nievo - 21220
   D. Stony -38890

2. Code No. 101002-R5527-U5007 2.____

   A. Nievo - 21220
   B. Haley - 39670
   C. Monte - 39213
   D. Claridge - 81927

3. Code No. 101003-R5527-U5007 3.____

   A. Nievo - 21220
   B. Monte - 39213
   C. Nievo - 12122
   D. Nievo - 21120

4. Code No. 110503-R5725-U5201 4.____

A. Nievo - 12122
B. Nievo - 21220
C. Haley - 39670
D. Stony - 38390

5. Code No. 070102-R2275-U2175 5.____

A. Stony - 33890
B. Stony - 83930
C. Stony - 38390
D. Nievo - 21120

6. Code No. 120902-R3880-U380 6.____

A. Stony - 83930
B. Stony - 38890
C. Stony - 33890
D. Monte - 39213

Questions 7-10.

DIRECTIONS: Using the same chart, answer Questions 7 through 10 by choosing the letter (A, B, C, or D) in which the code number corresponds to the supplier and stock number given.

7. Nieve - 38903 7.____

A. 851903-R1733-U1703
B. 080502-R1733-U1703
C. 080503-R1733-U1703
D. 050803-R1733-U1703

8. Nevo - 47101 8.____

A. 081503-R9721-U8207
B. 091503-R9721-U8207
C. 110602-R485-U231
D. 061102-R485-U231

9. Dinal - 54921 9.____

A. 020403-R1711-U1117
B. 030202-R1171-U717
C. 020302-R1171-U717
D. 421903-R1711-U1117

10. Nievo - 21122 10.____

A. 070602-R4878-U3492
B. 060702-R4878-U349
C. 761902-R4878-U3492
D. 060702-R4878-U3492

KEY (CORRECT ANSWERS)

1. D
2. C
3. A
4. A
5. D

6. A
7. D
8. C
9. A
10. A

ARITHMETIC

EXAMINATION SECTION
TEST 1

DIRECTIONS: Each question or incomplete statement is followed by several suggested answers or completions. Select the one that BEST answers the question or completes the statement. *PRINT THE LETTER OF THE CORRECT ANSWER IN THE SPACE AT THE RIGHT.*

1. From 30983 subtract 29998. The answer should be 1.____

   A. 985 B. 995 C. 1005 D. 1015

2. From $2537.75 subtract $1764.28. The answer should be 2.____

   A. $763.58 B. $773.47 C. $774.48 D. $873.58

3. From 254211 subtract 76348. The answer should be 3.____

   A. 177863 B. 177963 C. 187963 D. 188973

4. Divide 4025 by 35. The answer should be 4.____

   A. 105 B. 109 C. 115 D. 125

5. Multiply 0.35 by 2764. The answer should be 5.____

   A. 997.50 B. 967.40 C. 957.40 D. 834.40

6. Multiply 1367 by 0.50. The answer should be 6.____

   A. 6.8350 B. 68.350 C. 683.50 D. 6835.0

7. Multiply 841 by 0.01. The answer should be 7.____

   A. 0.841 B. 8.41 C. 84.1 D. 841

8. Multiply 1962 by 25. The answer should be 8.____

   A. 47740 B. 48460 C. 48950 D. 49050

9. Multiply 905 by 0.05. The answer should be 9.____

   A. 452.5 B. 45.25 C. 4.525 D. 0.4525

10. Multiply 8.93 by 4.7. The answer should be 10.____

    A. 41.971 B. 40.871 C. 4.1971 D. 4.0871

11. Multiply 25 by 763. The answer should be 11.____

    A. 18075 B. 18875 C. 19075 D. 20965

12. Multiply 2530 by 0.10. The answer should be 12.____

    A. 2.5300 B. 25.300 C. 253.00 D. 2530.0

13. Multiply 3053 by 0.25. The answer should be 13.____

A. 76.325 B. 86.315 C. 763.25 D. 863.15

14. Multiply 6204 by 0.35. The answer should be 14.____

A. 2282.40 B. 2171.40 C. 228.24 D. 217.14

15. Multiply $.35 by 7619. The answer should be 15.____

A. $2324.75 B. $2565.65 C. $2666.65 D. $2756.75

16. Multiply 6513 by 45. The answer should be 16.____

A. 293185 B. 293085 C. 292185 D. 270975

17. Multiply 3579 by 70. The answer should be 17.____

A. 25053.0 B. 240530 C. 250530 D. 259530

18. A class had an average of 24 words correct on a spelling test. The class average on this spelling test was 80%.
The AVERAGE number of words missed on this test was 18.____

A. 2 B. 4 C. 6 D. 8

19. In which one of the following is 24 renamed as a product of primes? 19.____

A. 2 x 6 x 2
B. 8 x 3 x 1
C. 2 x 2 x 3 x 2
D. 3 x 4 x 2

Questions 20-23.

DIRECTIONS: In answering Questions 20 through 23, perform the indicated operation. Select the BEST answer from the choices below.

20. Add: 20.____

7068
2807
9434
6179

A. 26,488 B. 24,588 C. 25,488 D. 25,478

21. Divide: $75\overline{)45555}$ 21.____

A. 674 B. 607.4 C. 6074 D. 60.74

22. Multiply: 22.____

907
x806

A. 73,142 B. 13,202 C. 721,042 D. 731,042

23. Subtract: 23.____

60085
-47194

A. 12,891 B. 13,891 C. 12,991 D. 12,871

24. A librarian reported that 1/5% of all books taken out last school year had not been returned. 24.____
If 85,000 books were borrowed from the library, how many were not returned?

A. 170 B. 425 C. 1,700 D. 4,250

25. At 40 miles per hour, how many minutes would it take to travel 12 miles? 25.____

A. 30 B. 18 C. 15 D. 20

KEY (CORRECT ANSWERS)

1.	A	11.	C
2.	B	12.	C
3.	A	13.	C
4.	C	14.	B
5.	B	15.	C
6.	C	16.	B
7.	B	17.	C
8.	D	18.	C
9.	B	19.	C
10.	A	20.	C

21.	B
22.	D
23.	A
24.	A
25.	B

SOLUTIONS TO PROBLEMS

1. 30,983 - 29,998 = 985
2. $2537.75 - $1764.28 = $773.47
3. 254,211 - 76,348 = 177,863
4. 4025 ÷ 35 = 115
5. (.35)(2764) = 967.4
6. (1367)(.50) = 683.5
7. (841)(.01) = 8.41
8. (1962)(25) = 49,050
9. (905)(.05) = 45.25
10. (8.93)(4.7) = 41.971
11. (25)(763) = 19,075
12. (2530)(.10) = 253
13. (3053)(.25) = 763.25
14. (6204)(.35) = 2171.4
15. ($.35)(7619) = $2666.65
16. (6513)(45) = 293,085
17. (3579)(70) = 250,530
18. 24 ÷ .80 = 30. Then, 30 - 24 = 6 words
19. 24 = 2 x 2 x 3 x 2, where each number is a prime.
20. 7068 ÷ 2807 + 9434 + 6179 = 25,488
21. 45,555 ÷ 75 = 607.4
22. (907)(806) = 731,042
23. 60,085 - 47,194 = 12,891
24. (1/5%)(85,000) = (.002)(85,000) = 170 books
25. Let x = number of minutes. Then, $\frac{40}{60}=\frac{12}{x}$. Solving, x = 18

TEST 2

DIRECTIONS: Each question or incomplete statement is followed by several suggested answers or completions. Select the one that BEST answers the question or completes the statement. *PRINT THE LETTER OF THE CORRECT ANSWER IN THE SPACE AT THE RIGHT.*

1. The sum of 57901 + 34762 is 1.____
   A. 81663 B. 82663 C. 91663 D. 92663

2. The sum of 559 + 448 + 362 + 662 is 2.____
   A. 2121 B. 2031 C. 2021 D. 1931

3. The sum of 36153 + 28624 + 81379 is 3.____
   A. 136156 B. 146046 C. 146146 D. 146156

4. The sum of 742 + 9197 + 8972 is 4.____
   A. 19901 B. 18911 C. 18801 D. 17921

5. The sum of 7989 + 8759 + 2726 is 5.____
   A. 18455 B. 18475 C. 19464 D. 19474

6. The sum of $111.55 + $95.05 + $38.80 is 6.____
   A. $234.40 B. $235.30 C. $245.40 D. $254.50

7. The sum of 1302 + 46187 + 92610 + 4522 is 7.____
   A. 144621 B. 143511 C. 134621 D. 134521

8. The sum of 47953 + 58041 + 63022 + 22333 is 8.____
   A. 170248 B. 181349 C. 191349 D. 200359

9. The sum of 76563 + 43693 + 38521 + 50987 + 72723 is 9.____
   A. 271378 B. 282386 C. 282487 D. 292597

10. The sum of 85923 + 97211 + 11333 + 4412 + 22533 is 10.____
    A. 209302 B. 212422 C. 221412 D. 221533

11. The sum of 4299 + 54163 + 89765 + 1012 + 38962 is 11.____
    A. 188201 B. 188300 C. 188301 D. 189311

12. The sum of 48526 + 709 + 11534 + 80432 + 6096 is 12.____
    A. 135177 B. 139297 C. 147297 D. 149197

13. The sum of $407.62 + $109.01 + $68.44 + $378.68 is 13.____
    A. $963.75 B. $964.85 C. $973.65 D. $974.85

14. From 40614 subtract 4697. The answer should be 14.____

A. 35917 B. 35927 C. 36023 D. 36027

15. From 81773 subtract 5717. The answer should be 15.____

A. 75964 B. 76056 C. 76066 D. 76956

16. From $1755.35 subtract $1201.75. The answer should be 16.____

A. $542.50 B. $544.50 C. $553.60 D. $554.60

17. From $2402.10 subtract $998.85. The answer should be 17.____

A. $1514.35 B. $1504.25 C. $1413.25 D. $1403.25

18. Add: 18.____

12 1/2
2 1/2
3 1/2

A. 17 B. 17 1/4 C. 17 3/4 D. 18

19. Subtract: 19.____

150
-80

A. 70 B. 80 C. 130 D. 150

20. After cleaning up some lots in the city dump, five cleanup crews loaded the following amounts of garbage on trucks: 20.____

Crew No. 1 loaded 2 1/4 tons
Crew No. 2 loaded 3 tons
Crew No. 3 loaded 1 1/4 tons
Crew No. 4 loaded 2 1/4tons
Crew No. 5 loaded 1/2 ton.

The TOTAL number of tons of garbage loaded was

A. 8 1/4 B. 8 3/4 C. 9 D. 9 1/4

21. Subtract: 21.____

17 3/4
-7 1/4

A. 7 1/2 B. 10 1/2 C. 14 1/4 D. 17 3/4

22. Yesterday, Tom and Bill each received 10 leaflets about rat control. They were supposed to distribute one leaflet to each supermarket in the neighborhood. When the day was over, Tom had 8 leaflets left. Bill had no leaflets left. 22.____
How many supermarkets got leaflets yesterday?

A. 8 B. 10 C. 12 D. 18

23. What is 2/3 of 1 1/8? 23.____

A. 1 11/16 B. 3/4 C. 3/8 D. 4 1/3

24. A farmer bought a load of 120 bushels of corn. 24.____
After he fed 45 bushels to his hogs, what fraction of his supply remained?

A. 5/8 B. 3/5 C. 3/8 D. 4/7

25. In the numeral 3,159,217, the 2 is in the ______ column. 25.____

A. hundreds B. units C. thousands D. tens

KEY (CORRECT ANSWERS)

1. D
2. B
3. D
4. B
5. D
6. C
7. A
8. C
9. C
10. C
11. A
12. C
13. A
14. A
15. B
16. C
17. D
18. D
19. A
20. D
21. B
22. C
23. B
24. A
25. A

SOLUTIONS TO PROBLEMS

1. 57,901 + 34,762 = 92,663
2. 559 + 448 + 362 + 662 = 2031
3. 36,153 + 28,624 + 81,379 = 146,156
4. 742 + 9197 + 8972 = 18,911
5. 7989 + 8759 + 2726 = 19,474
6. $111.55 + $95.05 + $38.80 = $245.40
7. 1302 + 46,187 + 92,610 + 4522 = 144,621
8. 47,953 + 58,041 + 63,022 + 22,333 = 191,349
9. 76,563 + 45,693 + 38,521 + 50,987 + 72,723 = 282,487
10. 85,923 + 97,211 + 11,333 + 4412 + 22,533 = 221,412
11. 4299 + 54,163 + 89,765 + 1012 + 38,962 = 188,201
12. 48,526 + 709 + 11,534 + 80,432 + 6096 = 147,297
13. $407.62 + $109.01 + $68.44 + $378.68 = $963.75
14. 40,614 - 4697 = 35,917
15. 81,773 - 5717 = 76,056
16. $1755.35 - $1201.75 = $553.60
17. $2402.10 - $998.85 = $1403.25
18. 12 1/2 + 2 1/4 + 3 1/4 = 17 4/4 = 18
19. 150 - 80 = 70
20. 2 1/4 + 3 + 1 1/4 + 2 1/4 + 1/2 = 8 5/4 = 9 1/4 tons
21. 17 3/4 -7 1/4 = 10 2/4 = 10 1/2
22. 10 + 10 - 8 - 0 = 12 supermarkets
23. $(\frac{2}{3})(1\frac{1}{8}) = (\frac{2}{3})(\frac{9}{8}) = \frac{18}{24} = \frac{3}{4}$
24. 120 - 45 = 75. Then, $\frac{75}{120} = \frac{5}{8}$
25. The number 2 is in the hundreds column of 3,159,217

TEST 3

DIRECTIONS: Each question or incomplete statement is followed by several suggested answers or completions. Select the one that BEST answers the question or completes the statement. *PRINT THE LETTER OF THE CORRECT ANSWER IN THE SPACE AT THE RIGHT.*

1. The distance covered in three minutes by a subway train traveling at 30 mph is _______ mile(s). 1.____

   A. 3 B. 2 C. 1 1/2 D. 1

2. A crate contains 3 pieces of equipment weighing 73, 84, and 47 pounds, respectively. The empty crate weighs 16 pounds. If the crate is lifted by 4 trackmen, each trackman lifting one corner of the crate, the AVERAGE number of pounds lifted by each of the trackmen is 2.____

   A. 68 B. 61 C. 55 D. 51

3. The weight per foot of a length of square-bar 4" x 4" in cross-section, as compared with one 2" x 2" in cross-section, is ______ as much. 3.____

   A. twice B. 2 1/2 times
   C. 3 times D. 4 times

4. An order for 360 feet of 2" x 8" lumber is shipped in 20-foot lengths. The MAXIMUM number of 9-foot pieces that can be cut from this shipment is 4.____

   A. 54 B. 40 C. 36 D. 18

5. If a trackman gets $10.40 per hour and time and one-half for working over 40 hours, his gross salary for a week in which he worked 44 hours should be 5.____

   A. $457.60 B. $478.40 C. $499.20 D. $514.80

6. If a section of ballast 6'-0" wide, 8'-0" long, and 2'-6" deep is excavated, the amount of ballast removed is ______ cu. feet. 6.____

   A. 96 B. 104 C. 120 D. 144

7. The sum of 7'2 3/4", 0'-2 7/8", 3'-0", 4'-6 3/8", and 1'-9 1/4" is 7.____

   A. 16'-8 1/4" B. 16'-8 3/4" C. 16'-9 1/4" D. 16' -9 3/4"

8. The sum of 3 1/16", 4 1/4", 2 5/8", and 5 7/16" is 8.____

   A. 15 3/16" B. 15 1/4" C. 15 3/8" D. 15 1/2"

9. Add: $51.79, $29.39, and $8.98. The CORRECT answer is 9.____

   A. $78.97 B. $88.96 C. $89.06 D. $90.16

10. Add: $72.07 and $31.54. Then subtract $25.75. The CORRECT answer is 10.____

    A. $77.86 B. $82.14 C. $88.96 D. $129.36

11. Start with $82.47. Then subtract $25.50, $4.75, and 35¢. The CORRECT answer is 11.____

A. $30.60 B. $51.87 C. $52.22 D. $65.25

12. Add: $19.35 and $37.75. Then subtract $9.90 and $19.80. The CORRECT answer is 12.____

A. $27.40 B. $37.00 C. $37.30 D. $47.20

13. Add: 13.____

$$
\begin{array}{r}
\$153 \\
114 \\
210 \\
\underline{+186}
\end{array}
$$

A. $657 B. $663 C. $713 D. $757

14. Add: 14.____

$$
\begin{array}{r}
\$64.91 \\
13.53 \\
19.27 \\
20.00 \\
\underline{+72.84}
\end{array}
$$

A. $170.25 B. $178.35 C. $180.45 D. $190.55

15. Add: 15.____

$$
\begin{array}{r}
1963 \\
1742 \\
\underline{+2497}
\end{array}
$$

A. 6202 B. 6022 C. 5212 D. 5102

16. Add: 16.____

$$
\begin{array}{r}
206 \\
709 \\
1342 \\
\underline{+2076}
\end{array}
$$

A. 3432 B. 3443 C. 4312 D. 4333

17. Subtract: 17.____

$$
\begin{array}{r}
\$190.76 \\
\underline{-\quad .99}
\end{array}
$$

A. $189.97 B. $189.87 C. $189.77 D. $189.67

18. From 99876 subtract 85397. The answer should be 18.____

A. 14589 B. 14521 C. 14479 D. 13589

19. From $876.51 subtract $92.89. The answer should be 19.____

A. $773.52 B. $774.72 C. $783.62 D. $784.72

20. From 70935 subtract 49489. The answer should be 20.____

A. 20436 B. 21446 C. 21536 D. 21546

21. From $391.55 subtract $273.45. The answer should be 21.____

A. $118.10 B. $128.20 C. $178.10 D. $218.20

22. When 119 is subtracted from the sum of 2016 + 1634, the answer is 22.____

A. 2460 B. 3531 C. 3650 D. 3769

23. Multiply 35 x 65 x 15. The answer should be 23.____

A. 2275 B. 24265 C. 31145 D. 34125

24. Multiply: 4.06 24.____
x.031

A. 1.2586 B. .12586 C. .02586 D. .1786

25. When 65 is added to the result of 14 multiplied by 13, the answer is 25.____

A. 92 B. 182 C. 247 D. 16055

KEY (CORRECT ANSWERS)

1.	C	11.	B
2.	C	12.	A
3.	D	13.	B
4.	C	14.	D
5.	B	15.	A
6.	C	16.	D
7.	C	17.	C
8.	C	18.	C
9.	D	19.	C
10.	A	20.	B

21. A
22. B
23. D
24. B
25. C

SOLUTIONS TO PROBLEMS

1. Let x = distance. Then, $\frac{30}{60} = \frac{x}{3}$ Solving, x = 1 1/2 miles

2. (73 + 84 + 47 + 16) ÷ 4 = 55 pounds

3. (4 x 4) ÷ (2 x 2) = a ratio of 4 to 1.

4. 20 ÷ 9 = 2 2/9 , rounded down to 2 pieces. Then, (360 ÷ 20)(2) = 36

5. Salary =($10.40)(40) + ($15.60)(4) = $478.40

6. (6)(8)(2 1/2) = 120 cu.ft.

7. $7'2\frac{3}{4}"+0'2\frac{7}{8}"+3'0"+4'6\frac{3}{8}"+1'9\frac{1}{4}"=15'19\frac{18}{8}"=15'21\frac{1}{4}"=16'9\frac{1}{4}"$

8. $3\frac{1}{16}"+4\frac{1}{4}"+2\frac{5}{8}"+5\frac{7}{16}"=14\frac{22}{16}"=15\frac{3}{8}"$

9. $51.79 + $29.39 + $8.98 = $90.16

10. $72.07 + $31.54 = $103.61. Then, $103.61 - $25.75 = $77.86

11. $82.47 - $25.50 - $4.75 - $0.35 = $51.87

12. $19.35 + $37.75 = $57.10. Then, $57.10 - $9.90 - $19.80 = $27.40

13. $153 + $114 + $210 + $186 = $663

14. $64.91 + $13.53 + $19.27 + $20.00 + $72.84 = $190.55

15. 1963 + 1742 + 2497 = 6202

16. 206 + 709 + 1342 + 2076 = 4333

17. $190.76 - .99 = $189.77

18. 99,876 - 85,397 = 14,479

19. $876.51 - $92.89 = $783.62

20. 70,935 - 49,489 = 21,446

21. $391.55 - $273.45 = $118.10

22. (2016 + 1634) - 119 = 3650 - 119 = 3531

23. (35)(65)(15) = 34,125

24. (4.06)(.031) = .12586

25. 65 + (14)(13) = 65 + 182 = 247

www.ingramcontent.com/pod-product-compliance
Lightning Source LLC
Chambersburg PA
CBHW082205300426
44117CB00016B/2678